REDUCTION
in the
ABSTRACT
SCIENCES

Winner of the 1980 Johnsonian Prize

Daniel A. Bonevac

REDUCTION
in the
ABSTRACT
SCIENCES

with a Foreword by
Wilfrid Sellars

HACKETT PUBLISHING COMPANY
Indianapolis • Cambridge

Printed in the United States of America

For further information, please address
Hackett Publishing Company, Inc.
P.O. Box 55573
Indianapolis, IN 46205

Library of Congress Cataloging in Publication Data

Bonevac, Daniel A., 1955-
Reduction in the abstract sciences.

Includes bibliographical references and index.
1. Science—Theory reduction. 2. Ontology. 3. Knowledge, Theory of. I. Title.
Q175.B715   111   81–6775
ISBN 0–915145–14–6   AACR2

CONTENTS

FOREWORD

Dr. Leigh S. Cauman

Journal of Philosophy

720 Philosophy Hall

Columbia University

New York, New York   10027

August 28, 1980

Dear Dr. Cauman:

Dan Bonevac's dissertation on "Ontological Reduction and Abstract Entities" is undoubtedly the finest I have read, let alone directed, in the past decade.

The aim of the dissertation can be briefly characterized as that of establishing adequacy conditions for a reduction of abstract to non-abstract entities. This involves a careful exploration of current accounts of what it is to 'reduce' one domain of objects to another. It also requires an examination of the sense in which a reduced object might be 'identical' with a set of reducing objects. In other words it involves a discussion of inter-theoretic identity. On both these topics Bonevac has fresh and illuminating things to say. His analysis of recent attempts to define a concept of 'relative identity' is particularly incisive and merits publication in its own right.

Bonevac takes numbers as his paradigm of abstract entities. Thus the specifics of his argument begin with a careful account of controversies in the ontology of number theory. He takes as his point of departure Benacerraf's puzzle as to how to fit together into one coherent story the semantical and the epistemological dimensions of arithmetic. Bonevac, as indicated above, expands the puzzle to include abstract entities generally, and emphasizes that by the 'epistemological' dimension he has in mind the cognitive psychology of thinking about the abstract. The cumulative force of his examination of patterns of reduction is to show that a crucial, if neglected, adequacy condition for a reduction of abstract entities is to be found at the intersection of ontology with the philosophy of mind. It is, of course, no flaw in the dissertation that no ontological reduction of abstract entities is actually undertaken or even sketched, though our appetite for such an attempt has

1

indeed been whetted. The magnitude of the task is both familiar and awesome. The time for promissory notes is surely over. It is, therefore, a major achievement on Bonevac's part to have clarified the nature of the enterprise to an extent which means that those who undertake it (and he proposes to be one) will be in a position to recognize when they have pulled it off.

Bonevac writes with a clear and free-flowing style. He discusses highly technical issues without resorting to jargon or to restatements which paraphrase without illuminating. The argument is truly philosophical in spirit. There is no lingering over formalisms for their own sake. Yet when the argument calls for rigor it is there, and Bonevac makes it clear, without flaunting the fact, that he is thoroughly at home in as demanding a subject-matter as there is in philosophy today.

To sum up: In my opinion the dissertation deals with a family of issues of major importance, deals with them clearly, and in such a manner as to bring out their philosophical significance. Within its terms of reference, the argument succeeds. All in all a most impressive piece of work.

Sincerely yours,

WILFRID SELLARS
University Professor
of Philosophy
University of Pittsburgh

PREFACE

My objective in writing this book is to articulate a comprehensive and correct analysis of ontological reduction concerning theories with ostensible commitments to abstract objects. Discourse seeming to involve commitments to such objects creates tension between semantics and epistemology, for it seems that we cannot have any epistemic contact with abstract entities. How can we account for the truth of such discourse, without settling for a metaphor as our theory of knowledge or entirely reconstructing the theory of truth? I attempt to eliminate reference to abstract objects in mathematics and other abstract sciences by employing a linguistic concept of reduction based not on identifying objects but on eliminating and replacing theories.

A linguistic account of reduction, though often considered, has rarely been adopted. Noting that, in abstract sciences such as mathematics, problematic theories can generally be reduced to other theories in more than one way, Paul Benacerraf has argued that reduction in the abstract sciences can have no ontological significance. How could it be meaningful to identify the number 1 as a set, he asks, if we are not willing to identify it with a unique, particular set? W. V. Quine, too, rejects a linguistic account because of the Löwenheim-Skolem theorem, which threatens to permit the reduction of any theory to a theory of numbers. I defend the linguistic theory by constructing a semantics for intertheoretic identity statements, demonstrating *contra* Benacerraf that intertheoretic sentences are meaningful even in cases of multiple reduction and that the approach to identity underlying my semantics has much to recommend it on more general philosophical grounds. I further demonstrate that a linguistic criterion of success in reduction, when taken against a broader background, allays Quine's fear of a world of numbers without employing anything analogous to proxy functions.

Finally, I present a theory of ontological commitment. I distinguish ostensible commitment, closely linked to existential quantification, from real commitment, which takes reductive relations into account. The theory leads to a distinction between linguistic and nonlinguistic problems in ontology and to the formulation of an epistemological criterion

3

for making decisions about our ultimate ontological commitments.

The theory of reduction I am advocating has several significant implications. First, though my account is developed in counterpoint with Carnap and Quine, I contend that we have epistemological—and so theoretical, not merely pragmatic—reasons for endowing some reductions with ontological significance and withholding such distinction from others. Second, my analysis implies that the resolution of ontological issues requires the employment of epistemological as well as logical or linguistic considerations. Ontological questions can be answered only partially by appeals to the structure of our language; the questions that remain must be settled by examining the structure and indeed the content of our theories of knowledge acquisition.

Third, my account of reduction provides the nominalist a program for the elimination of reference to abstract entities. The book is in this sense an ontological prelude to a program of constructing most of our theories from a basis consisting only of theories the commitments of which are acceptable to the nominalist.

Nominalism, of course, is an ontological project, yet also a negative one; it provides a partial answer to What is there? by detailing what there is *not*. But once we accept the sometimes methodological, sometimes substantive thesis of much contemporary ontology—that we can best discover what there is by learning about what our theories or linguistic usages countenance or commit us to—we can see that the fundamental thesis of nominalism splits into two principles. First, the nominalist must show that we do not need to countenance abstract objects; he must demonstrate that we can avoid commitments to them without disrupting essential theories and usages. The account of reduction I develop gives the nominalist a method for doing exactly this. Second, he has to show that we *must* avoid commitments to abstract objects. It is not enough to show that it is possible to refuse to countenance abstract entities; the nominalist must show that it is necessary to refuse to countenance them. Unless we can demonstrate that we need to do without abstract objects, nominalistic reconstructions of ordinary or scientific discourse will be as interesting to the philosopher as feasibility studies on iceberg towing might be to the mayor of Seattle. To put the point differently, the nominalist needs a philosophical argument for the principle that we should avoid commitments to abstract objects. Standard appeals to "an intuition that cannot be justified." Occam's razor, a love of parsimony, or a taste for desert landscapes have at best an aesthetic force. The philosopher with different intuitions and the lover of jungles, beards, and Platonic richness can always plead *de gustibus non disputandum.*

What can be reduced to what? is a purely ontological question—a question of *reducibility*, I shall say—calling for a purely linguistic response. The nominalist can demonstrate his first principle, then, by strictly logical means, given a set of theories we accept as descriptions of the world. But What should be reduced to what? is a broadly epistemological question—a question of *primacy*—calling for a response that goes beyond ontology to, among other things, our best theories of knowledge acquisition. The nominalist can therefore argue that we should not countenance abstract objects by arguing that we cannot acquire knowledge of them.

I argue, therefore, that since we must be able to have epistemic contact with the objects to which we commit ourselves ontologically, we must refuse to countenance abstract entities. This move assumes that abstract objects are not epistemically accessible to us, i.e., that we have no empirically scrutable relation to them. By 'empirically scrutable relation' I mean a relation we might in principle expect to uncover and explain through empirical scientific investigation. As the reader will soon learn, however, I simply take the empirical inscrutability of abstract objects as an assumption throughout the course of this work. A full justification of this assumption would require an examination of our empirical theories of cognition and some philosophical reflection on the nature of a cognitive science in general. The nominalist must supplement my analysis, then, with such a justification. His opponent, of course, may find my account just as useful, for if no such justification can be provided we have no reason to reject commitments to abstract entities on principle.

Though I begin with a dilemma concerning the truth of theories involving commitments to abstract objects, I fall short of resolving the dilemma in this book. A true resolution of the sort I have in mind would cement the above-mentioned gap by justifying my assertion of the empirical inscrutability of our relations with abstract objects. It would also apply the reductive technique I characterize and defend to the actual reduction of theories with abstract commitments (most notably, set theory) to those without them. Only after these additional projects are completed will we be able to say that reference to abstract objects, which gives rise to the dilemma concerning truth, has been eliminated. This book is thus nothing more than a first step—but an essential step—toward the establishment of harmony between ontology and epistemology.

For the weaknesses of this book—and for what are, I hope, some of its strengths—I take full responsibility. But many people have contributed their time and talents to improving the manuscript. Carl Hempel, Kenneth Manders, Kenneth Schaffner, and Carl Posy read several drafts in their entirety and made many helpful suggestions. Ermanno Bencivenga read earlier versions of chapters five and six, assisting me in removing some confusions. I benefited also from conversations with Nicholas Rescher, Leslie Tharp, Robert Kraut, and Willem de Vries.

I am profoundly and especially indebted to two others, who devoted a great deal of energy to working with me during the writing of this book. Wilfrid Sellars served as an invaluable guide and critic; those familiar with his work will recognize his impact in many more places than the notes might indicate. Gerald Massey helped me to outline the project as a whole and then scrutinized my execution of it in great substantive and stylistic detail. Many of the insights of this book can no doubt be traced to the contributions of one or both of these philosophers.

I would also like to thank the editorial staff of *The Journal of Philosophy* and, in particular, Charles D. Parsons. Their criticisms, corrections, and suggestions have done much to improve the book in both content and presentation. I am indebted too to Hackett Publishing Company for its kind assistance and support.

I want to thank the University of Pittsburgh, to which I submitted an earlier version of this book as my doctoral dissertation, *Ontological Reduction and Abstract Entities*, in April of 1980. The University provided me financial support and the use of its DEC-10 computer, the true hero of this work, which greatly facilitated the writing and editing of the manuscript. I am grateful to the University and the people of Pittsburgh for providing a very nearly ideal intellectual environment—full of excitement, yet empty of pretense—throughout my work on this project.

Finally, I owe thanks to all those individuals—especially Lily Knezevich, Jack Fuchs, my brother James—and, above all, my wife Beverly—who gave me their personal support and their friendship.

1 Reduction and Abstract Objects

Paul Benacerraf has articulated a dilemma concerning the nature of mathematical truth which has resulted in a cascade of research in the philosophy of mathematics.[1] Benacerraf's dilemma generates a certain tension between ontology and epistemology which afflicts attempts to provide a satisfying account of mathematical truth. I shall argue that this tension plagues accounts of truth in general. In particular, I shall argue that we can generate Benacerraf's dilemma from assumptions weaker than those to which he commits himself and that the dilemma essentially concerns not mathematical truth but abstract entities. Finally I shall contend that, if we accept my weaker assumptions, ontological reduction offers us a route, indeed the only route, for escaping the dilemma.

1. The Dilemma

Benacerraf has noted that we can account adequately for either the truth conditions of mathematical sentences or the knowledge of mathematical truths but not both. As he explains the problem,

> . . . accounts of truth that treat mathematical and non-mathematical discourse in relevantly similar ways do so at the cost of leaving it unintelligible how we can have any mathematical knowledge whatsoever; whereas those which attribute to mathematical propositions the kinds of truth conditions we can clearly know to obtain, do so

---

1. "Mathematical Truth," *Journal of Philosophy*, LXX, 19 (Nov. 8, 1973): 661–679; parenthetical page references will be to this paper, unless otherwise noted. For examples of research inspired by Benacerraf's article, see Mark Steiner, *Mathematical Knowledge* (Ithaca, N.Y.: Cornell, 1975), and "Mathematics, Explanation, and Scientific Knowledge," *Noûs*, XXII, 1 (March 1978): 17–28; Glenn Paul Kessler, *Numbers, Truth, and Knowledge* (Ph.D. dissertation, Princeton University, 1976); Michael Jubien, "Ontology and Mathematical Truth," *Noûs*, XI, 2 (May 1977): 133–150; Richard Grandy, "In Defense of a Modest Platonism," *Philosophical Studies*, XXXII, 4 (November 1977): 359–369; Jonathan Lear, "Sets and Semantics," *Journal of Philosophy*, LXXIV, 2 (February 1977): 86–102; Michael D. Resnik, "Mathematical Knowledge and Pattern Cognition," *Canadian Journal of Philosophy*, V, 1 (1975): 25–39; W. D. Hart, "On an Argument for Formalism," *Journal of Philosophy*, LXXI, 2 (Jan. 31, 1974): 29–46; Philip Kitcher,"The Plight of the Platonist," *Noûs*, XI, 2 (May 1978): 119–136; and Leslie Tharp, "Myth and Mathematics," to appear.

> at the expense of failing to connect these conditions with any analysis of the sentences which shows how the assigned conditions are conditions of their *truth* (662).

Benacerraf generates this dilemma from two assumptions: that we ought to maintain a unified, Tarskian semantics for the entire body of our discourse, and that we ought to hold a causal theory of knowledge. Two weaker assumptions serve to do the same work; I shall state them, but not argue for them here, since each presupposes the resolution of some rather complicated issues. My first assumption is that we ought to explain truth, semantically, in terms of reference and satisfaction. Tarski's semantics presents a paradigm of such an account, though I do not assume that it is the correct one, if there is any unique "correct" one; nor do I assume that any single account must serve the entire body of our discourse. *How* we link truth with reference and satisfaction, in other words, I leave an open question. I require, however, that there be *some* such link. This assumption demands that we take semantics seriously from an ontological point of view, in the sense that determinations of truth value must, in general, depend upon extralinguistic objects and their characteristics. We can expect, consequently, some sentences to commit us to the existence of an object, and, in particular, some theories to commit us to collections of objects, in the sense that semantic analysis may indicate that the sentences can be true only if some object or objects exist. Quantification, and especially existential quantification, provides a vehicle for making such commitments explicit within a theory. I shall therefore focus on existential sentences in speaking of the ontological commitments of a theory.

My second assumption is that we ought to have *epistemic access* to the objects we take our discourse to be about. That is, there must be some possibility of epistemic contact between us and these objects, which can explain our possession of knowledge about them; in Benacerraf's words, we must have "an account of the link between our cognitive faculties and the objects known" (674). By requiring "epistemic access" I mean to demand that any connection postulated between ourselves and the objects of knowledge must allow for the possibility of an empirical cognitive psychology, or even a cognitive physiology. In short, our ability to have knowledge concerning the objects assumed to exist must itself be capable of being a subject for empirical, and preferably phys-

iological, investigation. Benacerraf makes a stronger requirement: that a causal link connect the knower and the objects of knowledge. A real causal link of this nature, of course,
satisfies my requirement, but I do not assume that nothing
but a causal relationship can provide such a link. I demand
only that there be an empirically scrutable relationship that
grounds our claims to knowledge of objects.

This assumption rules out as illegitimate accounts of
knowledge like those of Kurt Gödel, or extreme rationalists,
who postulate a special faculty of intuition, "something like a
perception,"[2] which relates us to abstract objects and enables
us to apprehend abstract truths. Wilfrid Sellars has called this
approach the "Canadian mountie" theory of knowledge,
since it requires "immediate apprehension" of the objects of
knowledge. But such an account explains no more, or less,
than does Molière's doctor when he says that opium causes
sleep because of its "dormitive virtue." In short, a "Canadian
mountie" view, to account for our knowledge of abstract
truths, simply postulates an ability to acquire such knowledge without grounding this ability in empirically scrutable
relationships.

My two assumptions, I claim, suffice to allow us to reconstruct Benacerraf's dilemma. Furthermore, this reconstruction will demonstrate that the dilemma, in essence, concerns
not mathematical truth but abstract entities and claims of
knowledge about them. Let us begin, nevertheless, by focusing on knowledge claims in mathematics.

From a semantical point of view, no difficulty would arise
if we could treat mathematics as dealing "with very simple
and general things, without bothering about their existence
or non-existence,"[3] as Descartes did; what creates the problem is that mathematics does make existence claims. In set
theory, we find the axiom of infinity, asserting the existence
of an infinite multitude of sets; on a more basic level, we
come upon the null-set axiom, also existential in force. In
number theory, we find theorems asserting the existence of
infinitely many primes. Thus W. V. Quine has held that clas-

---

2. "Russell's Mathematical Logic," in Benacerraf and Hilary Putnam, eds.,
Philosophy of Mathematics (Englewood Cliffs, N.J.: Prentice-Hall, 1964), p.
220; also "What Is Cantor's Continuum Problem," in *op. cit.*, pp. 263, 272.
My account of Gödel's theory of knowledge is simplified slightly, but in
ways that do not affect the point at issue.

3. *Meditations, I*, F. E. Sutcliffe trans. (New York: Penguin, 1968), p. 98.

sical mathematics "is up to its neck in commitments to an ontology of abstract entities."[4]

These existence claims force the philosopher interested in providing a semantics for mathematical discourse to make a choice: in Benacerraf's terms, he can choose either to offer a semantical account that maintains continuity between mathematical and nonmathematical language, or attempt to interpret mathematical sentences as radically different, semantically, from those nonmathematical sentences to which they bear a superficial resemblance. If, however, we accept my first assumption—that truth must be explained semantically in terms of reference and satisfaction—then, whether our treatment of mathematical discourse conforms to that accorded the rest of language or not, we must postulate entities (numbers, sets, or whatever else seems appropriate), the existence of which explicates or justifies the truth of the existential sentences in mathematics.

This is the approach taken by platonism; more generally, I think, it is the approach taken by *contensivism*, the view that mathematics has a definite subject matter, that mathematical objects, in some sense or other, exist, and that mathematical statements are true or false insofar as they agree or disagree with the facts about these objects.[5] The view that we should analyze mathematical truth along the lines of a correspondence theory of truth thus lies at the heart of contensivism; a referential semantics, therefore, fits nicely into the program. Of course, not all contensivists are platonists, holding that the objects about which mathematical language speaks do not depend upon mental activity; many intuitionists, too, hold that truth in mathematics is correspondence with the facts about some realm of objects, that is, mental mathematical constructions, though these objects do depend on mental activity, and though intuitionists differ from platonists in their account of what it is to be an object.

Contensivism runs into difficulty, unfortunately, in a way absolutely central to its own program. The correspondence theory of truth, when applied to mathematical language, requires the postulation of a realm of entities; these entities, by their very nature, create problems for epistemology. Though

4. "On What There Is," in *From a Logical Point of View* (New York: Harper & Row, 1961): 1–19, p. 13.

5. Haskell B. Curry, *Foundations of Mathematical Logic* (New York: Dover, 1977), p. 8. 'Contensive' was coined by Curry to translate the German 'inhaltlich'.

the contensivist can explain what he takes truth in mathematics to be (namely, correspondence), he cannot explain how it is that we have any knowledge of mathematical truth. Numbers, sets, and the other entities to which mathematics may appear to be committed, are things we cannot perceive directly; indeed, it appears that we stand in no causal, or otherwise empirically scrutable, contact whatever with them. But then how do we have any knowledge of them? Gödel, as we have seen, responds that we have a faculty of intuition which relates us to abstract objects; many intuitionists likewise hold that we have the ability to introspect and to intuit the nature of our mental mathematical constructions, thus holding that mathematical objects exist, and have properties, only insofar as we have constructed them to have such properties.[6] The contensivist, then, tends to invoke a "Canadian mountie" theory of knowledge which carries little explanatory power. For platonism, and for contensivism in general, epistemology remains "a mysterious metaphor."[7]

Suppose, then, that the interpreter of mathematics opts for a construal of mathematical discourse as radically discontinuous with the semantics for the rest of language. Benacerraf contends that this is problematic in itself; what guarantees that the conception of truth which issues from such an account of mathematical truth is really an account of *truth* at all? One would need a more general account of truth—a "theory of truth theories," as Benacerraf says—to relate the correspondence theory of truth, which applies to most of our discourse, to a noncorrespondence theory of mathematical truth and to show that both of these conceptions are legitimate varieties of truth (666).

This, of course, is not a *reductio* but a challenge. The challenge can, in principle, be met if we accept my weaker assumptions; for we might explain truth in terms of reference in several different ways in different parts of the language. My first assumption thus assails nonreferential, rather than merely discontinuous, semantical approaches. We have seen that the adoption of a referential semantics seems to create problems for epistemology; we can now show that the adoption of a nonreferential semantics, in its most common form, fares no better.

Typically, those who have denied that mathematical state-

6. Arend Heyting, "The Intuitionist Foundations of Mathematics," in Benacerraf and Putnam, *op. cit.*, p. 42.

7. Resnik, *op. cit.*, p. 30.

ments should be interpreted referentially have adhered to *formalism*. A formalist holds that mathematics has no definite subject matter, except perhaps for its own symbolism; he denies that any characteristically mathematical objects exist; and he holds that if mathematical statements are to be considered true or false at all, it is certainly not because they correspond, or fail to correspond, to the facts.

Most frequently, formalists have identified truth with derivability in some formal system. We can know truths, then, simply because we can determine theoremhood; indeed, this kind of epistemological consideration has generally motivated formalism in the first place. But what is the connection—the philosophical connection, that is—between truth and theoremhood in a formal system? Benacerraf makes the point that formalists have not explained this, though they sorely need to do so. But we have reason to doubt that a formalist can explain any such connection. Gödel's incompleteness results have shown that there is no formal system for any reasonably strong portion of mathematics in which every true statement is provable, unless it is a system in which some false statements can be proved as well.[8] Thus we cannot identify truth with provability in any fairly powerful formal system. Some formalists have responded by holding that mathematics is not a formal system in itself, but the science of formal systems in general, including metatheoretical results concerning them, such as the theorems of Gödel. So, they have insisted, formalism can escape the specter of the incompleteness results;[9] truth in the object language can be identified with provability in the metalanguage, rather than in the object language itself. But if the metatheory is suitably formalized, then we cannot identify truth with provability in this formalization; if not, then the epistemological benefit of the original identification no longer remains, for now the metatheory is in need of a semantics. In short, the difficulties concerning the identification of truth with provability in the object language recur in the metalanguage.

In summary, then, my two assumptions suffice to show that accounts of mathematical truth which adequately explain the

---

8. "On Formally Undecidable Propositions of *Principia Mathematica* and Related Systems, I," in Jean van Heijenoort, *From Frege to Gödel: A Sourcebook in Mathematical Logic, 1879–1931* (Cambridge, Mass: Harvard, 1967): 592–618.

9. Curry, "Remarks on the Definition and Nature of Mathematics," in Benacerraf and Putnam, p. 154.

semantics of mathematical discourse do not explain mathematical knowledge, whereas those accounts which are designed to explain mathematical knowledge do not account for the nature of mathematical truth in a satisfying way. Thus the semantics and the epistemology of mathematics pull the philosopher in opposite directions; it seems that we cannot meet Benacerraf's demand that "an acceptable semantics for mathematics must fit an acceptable epistemology" (667).

Though this dilemma concerning mathematical truth has stirred up a great deal of interest within the philosophy of mathematics, it has hardly been noticed by philosophers outside that area. But if we examine the construction of the dilemma from my two assumptions, we find little employment of anything peculiar to mathematics. I claim, therefore, that this dilemma afflicts abstract objects and theories of truth in general.

I have already mentioned that the problems articulated by Benacerraf stem from the existential nature of some of the propositions of mathematics. Existential sentences involving ordinary physical objects do not present the same difficulties, because the ontological assumption that such objects exist does not stir up very great controversy and because we do seem to have some causal contact with these objects, so our knowledge of them is not utterly mysterious. But not all nonmathematical existence claims pertain to physical objects. In particular, some existential sentences seem, at first glance, to commit us to abstract entities, even though these sentences are not in the least mathematical. But all we needed in order to generate difficulties concerning mathematical truth was that a theory, when given a referential semantics, ostensibly commit us to the existence of abstract entities; entities, that is, with which we stand in no empirically scrutable relationship. To account for the truth of *any* such theory we must either reject a referential semantics or postulate a special faculty relating us to the objects of the theory. But each of these strategies violates one of my assumptions; we have thus constructed a dilemma concerning truth for any theory involving ostensible commitment to abstract objects.

Theories I have in mind might contain sentences such as:

There is something that Jones is. (e.g., "a man")
There is something that this exemplifies. (e.g., "triangularity")
There is a proposition that Jones believes. (e.g., "that Chicago is large")

There is a possibility that this argument will fail.
There is a contrast that must be mentioned.
There is a difficulty in that position.

Such theories ostensibly commit us to kinds, attributes, propositions, possibilities, contrasts, and difficulties, all of which are abstract objects, in some sense of that term; all are abstract at least to the extent that it is difficult to see how we might have any sort of epistemic contact with them. Now if we maintain a referential semantics with regard to these theories and hold that their truth is to be explained in terms of their correspondence with the facts about some realm of entities, we sanction these commitments and, thus, relegate to the inexplicable the knowledge we do have about propositions, possibilities, and the like. On the other hand, if we fashion an account of the truth of these theories which permits us to comprehend how we might have such knowledge, we must employ a nonreferential semantics and, thus, find ourselves faced with the problem of showing how this concept is really a concept of truth. In short, semantics and epistemology pull us in opposite directions whenever we are concerned with theories that ostensibly commit us to a realm of abstract entities.

Traditionally, rationalism has held that we should construe semantics for these theories, or theories similar to them, in close analogy with semantical treatments of theories involving commitments to physical objects. Thus the rationalist typically invokes a correspondence theory of truth and a realm of abstract objects to account for the truth of sentences seeming to carry a commitment to abstract entities. But, in the process, rationalism is forced to hold either that we have some special faculty of intuition that allows us direct epistemic contact with these objects—the "Canadian mountie" theory again—or that the objects, though important semantically, do not become involved in our acquisition of knowledge about them.

Empiricism, in contrast, has traditionally held that we should construe the semantics for discourse ostensibly involving commitments to abstract entities as quite distinct from the interpretation given more typical uses of language. Since we seem to have no experience of abstract objects and since the empiricist holds that all knowledge issues from experience, he must either deny that we have any knowledge of abstract objects (compare Hume on rationalistic metaphysics) or else insist that the discourse seeming to invoke them does not really force any such commitment (because, for example, they are only "trifling propositions"). The former course, though plausible at times, can hardly be maintained throughout all discourse that speaks of abstract entities; the latter course forces the empiricist to explain why the conception of truth he offers for those sentences, since it differs from the usual, referential account, is really an account of truth.

2. *Ontological Reduction*

Ontological reduction offers us a way—indeed the only way—of escaping the dilemma presented by the apparent disharmony between semantics and epistemology where ostensible commitments to abstract objects are concerned. To argue for a specific account of reduction here would take us too far into the subject matter of later chapters; I shall therefore presuppose the resolution of a number of issues and present my resulting view of ontological reduction.

Let us say that one theory is *reducible* to another just in case the first can be translated into the second, in such a way that the translation preserves predicate structure and theoremhood. To see how this pertains to the present problem, recall that the divergence of semantics and epistemology results from an ostensible commitment to abstract entities on the part of some statement or theory. Ontological reduction allows us to translate the theory ostensibly making such commitments into another theory that may not force the same commitments or, indeed, any commitments to abstract entities at all. In short, reduction gives us a way of showing that commitments can be avoided. If we can show that all the bits of discourse ostensibly making a problematic commitment can be avoided or eliminated, by way of translation into another theory making no such commitments, then we can show that the schism between semantics and epistemology can be avoided as well. Those sentences which seemed to force abstract objects upon us will now seem nothing more than *façons de parler* which we need not take seriously from an ontological point of view.

Consider, for example, the case of complex numbers. The notion of an imaginary number, and thus of a complex number, seems bizarre in itself; though introduced to simplify algebraic laws, these numbers were at first regarded with a great deal of suspicion. The suspicion dissolved with the demonstration that complex numbers can be reduced to pairs of real numbers. Anything we might say about complex numbers, therefore, can be translated into a statement about pairs of reals. The sentences that seemed to commit us to complex numbers as abstract objects thus turned out to be eliminable; complex numbers were consequently accepted as legitimate mathematical entities. Of course, the theory of real numbers also makes an ostensible commitment to abstract entities, and, in that sense, the above reduction does not remove all philosophical worry. But in most historical cases of reduction intended to have a similar impact, we distinguish between objects that we hold under suspicion, because they appear not to be epistemically accessible to us, and objects that we take to be well understood, typically because the reigning epistemology holds them to be epistemically tractable. Frege's reduction of arithmetic to logic had this character; whereas Hilbert was willing, at least sometimes, to assert existential sentences involving highly abstract objects on the basis of consistency, Frege felt the need to reduce questionable mathematical entities to more elementary ones.[10] Today we might find it peculiar that Frege held second-order logic, or set theory, to be better founded epistemologically than number theory, but he clearly thought of himself as reducing the truths of arithmetic to pure and self-evident truths of logic. The examples of the reduction of the theory of complex numbers to the theory of pairs of reals and of arithmetic to second-order logic or set theory indicate that reduction does not in itself demonstrate the epistemic accessibility of objects of a reduced theory, but instead establishes a *relative epistemic proximity* relation. We may say that a theory is *epistemically proximate* just in case the objects of that theory are epistemically accessible. These examples show that, if the theory of reals is epistemically proximate, in the sense that we have epistemic access to the objects to which that theory commits us, then so is the theory of complex numbers. Similarly, if second-order logic, or set theory, is epistemically proximate, then so is number theory. The reduction of a troublesome theory to another that does not give rise to dilemmas concerning truth may be indirect, that is, may proceed by way of a chain of intermediate reductions.

Examples of this sort extend far beyond mathematical contexts; as Quine has noticed, ontological reduction is "what we are most typically up to when in a philosophical spirit we offer an 'analysis' or 'explication' of some hitherto in-

10. Resnik, "The Frege-Hilbert Controversy," *Philosophy and Phenomenological Research*, XXXIV, 3 (March 1974): 394/5.

adequately formulated 'idea' or expression."[11] Of course, this is not invariably the case, for sometimes we intend philosophical analysis to clarify a previously unclear notion without the involvement of any question of ontological commitment. Nevertheless, many paradigm cases of analysis do fit the model of ontological reduction. Russell's theory of descriptions, for example, amounts to an attempt to show that we need not be committed to objects of a peculiar sort as denotations of what we now call "nondenoting singular terms," by showing how contexts that ostensibly commit us to such entities can be translated into language carrying no such commitment. Rudolf Carnap's attempt at translation of our discourse into a phenomenalistic language, based on a notion of "epistemic primacy," is a similar project; the nominalism of Nelson Goodman (and, upon occasion, Quine) also revolves around the attempt to translate discourse that seems to force a commitment to unacceptable entities into discourse that does not involve such commitments. As Goodman says, "the nominalist, after all, is looking for a nominalistic translation of everything that seems to him worth saving. . . . for we can use without qualms whatever we know how to eliminate."[12] Wilfrid Sellars, using a similar strategy, has shown that we can translate some of the sentences considered above ('There is an attribute that this exemplifies', for example) into sentences that no longer involve commitments to abstract entities.

Ontological reduction thus offers us a way to escape the seeming incompatibility of semantics and epistemology in cases of ostensible commitment to abstract entities. I shall argue for a stronger claim, however: if we accept my two assumptions, then ontological reduction offers us the only way to escape this dilemma. I shall isolate four strategies for dealing with theories involving ostensible commitments to abstract objects, and argue that only one of these strategies can satisfy us philosophically.

Strategy number one I shall call the *ostrich* strategy: we might just stop asserting the offending sentences of the troublesome theory and hope that our philosophical difficulties will go away. This rather blunt strategy does avoid commitments, for if we no longer assert a sentence as true, we need hardly worry about the nature of its commit-

11. *Word and Object* (Cambridge, Mass.: MIT Press, 1960), p. 258.

12. "A World of Individuals," in Benacerraf and Putnam, p. 206.

ments. But, in mathematics, the ostrich option is not very viable; it tosses the baby right out with the bath water, for not even the arithmetic of the integers can be constructed without existential assumptions.[13] In other abstract realms, too, this is likely to seem an unhappy choice, since some theories involving abstract terms are important—philosophical theories, for example—and since we generally think we have knowledge about propositions, contrasts, possibilities, and other abstract conceptions. To stop asserting any existential sentences that might commit us to these entities would amount to the admission that we are wrong to think we have such knowledge.

If we are to reject the ostrich strategy, we must face the ostensible commitments to abstract objects directly. We might, then consider strategy two: we can construct a nonreferential semantics for the offending theory. Assumption one, however, clearly precludes this possibility.

Given, then, that we want to maintain a referential semantics, we might opt for strategy three: we might construct what I shall call a *naively referential semantics* for the problematic theory. This strategy requires that we take the commitments of the theory at face value and accept the commitment to abstract objects which results. But these objects create problems for epistemology, as we have seen; we cannot explain our knowledge of them, for there is no empirically scrutable relationship linking them to our cognitive faculties. Strategy three, then, violates assumption two, by forcing us to rely upon a "Canadian mountie" theory of knowledge.

What alternative remains? We cannot hide from the troublesome commitments; we cannot employ a nonreferential semantics; we cannot employ a referential semantics committing us to abstract objects. All that is left is strategy four: to construct a referential semantics, but claim that the reference and, thus, the ontological commitment is not to abstract objects, but to objects to which we have epistemic access. To put the same option in a different way, we might show that we can stop asserting the troublesome theory, because its work can be performed by another theory that does not create the same problems. This, of course, is nothing but ontological reduction. To show that our theory, which ostensibly makes commitments to abstract entities, need not be as-

13. Ermanno Bencivenga, "Are Arithmetical Truths Analytic? New Results in Free Set Theory," *Journal of Philosophical Logic*, VI, 3 (August 1977): 319–330.

serted, we can demonstrate that the theory is eliminable, in the sense that any assertion of the theory can be translated into an assertion of another theory that does not give rise to the same epistemological problems. Thus sentences ostensibly referring to abstract objects can be paraphrased into sentences making no such ostensible reference. As a result, the dilemma concerning truth has no opportunity to arise; the dilemma stems from commitment to abstract objects, and ontological reduction demonstrates, ideally, that we can avoid such a commitment.

We have seen, then, that if two assumptions are accepted, a dilemma arises not only for mathematical truth but for any theory making ostensible reference to abstract entities. Furthermore, we have seen that ontological reduction is of considerable significance as a technique, indeed the only one, for bringing about an established—if not exactly preestablished—harmony between semantics and epistemology.

2 Philosophical Analysis and Construction

If the line of thinking reflected in the previous chapter is correct, then an analysis of the concept of reduction is crucial to the project of elucidating the nature of mathematical truth. The next several chapters will therefore attempt to outline an adequate account of reduction within the boundaries of a concern for theories involving an ostensible commitment to abstract objects. I say "outline" rather than "present" such an account, because I shall postpone certain problems until I can provide a more detailed treatment. Specifically, the difficulties that arise when one theory can be reduced to another in more than one way will concern chapter five, and the question of whether the specification of a "proxy function" is a necessary condition for ontological reduction I shall delay until chapter seven.

There is no single, widely accepted account of what a reduction from one theory to another is; indeed, a search for such an account tends to lead in many different directions. We will begin by looking to two of the early analysts of this century, Bertrand Russell and Rudolf Carnap, for insights embodied in their concepts of analysis and construction. This chapter, then, will consider accounts of reduction as a distinctly philosophical activity. In chapter three I shall consider reduction as a scientific activity, and then, in chapter four, as a mathematical activity useful for clarifying the relationships between formalized structures. Finally, I shall attempt to distill from these various perspectives a unified concept of ontological reduction.

1. *Logicism*

To one who seeks a formulation of reduction as a relationship between mathematical or otherwise abstract theories, logicism beckons as a natural starting point. The project of logicism, after all, is the reduction of mathematics to logic or, as we would be more likely to say today, to set theory, or second-order logic; furthermore, this reduction has been carried out successfully, in its mathematical aspects at least, owing largely to the work of Frege and of Russell and Whitehead in *Principia Mathematica*. Though philosophers may have substantial and well-grounded doubts about the success of logicism as a metaphysical or epistemological project, few have any doubt that, mathematically speaking, virtually all of classical mathematics can be reduced to set theory. Bourbaki, for example, remarks that "*on sait aujourd'hui qu'il est possible, logiquement parlant, de faire dériver presque toute la mathématique actuelle d'une source unique, la Théorie des Ensembles.*"[1] Logicism thus sparkles as a paradigm of reduction in mathematics.

We are interested, however, not in Russell and Whitehead's execution of the project, in all of its black-and-white detail, but rather in the underlying concept of reduction which this execution manifests. Unfortunately, Russell was not particularly reflective on the philosophical foundations of the logicist program; he had more interest in doing the actual work. It is necessary, therefore, to tease from his remarks on the over-all scheme of *Principia Mathematica* some general account of what a reduction is.

Russell's most typical statement of the logicist thesis is simply that mathematics *follows from* logic. Though this is vague, it suggests that the underlying notion of reduction is essentially *derivational*.[2] Commentators have almost invariably analyzed this thesis as consisting of two principles, as Russell himself does in the preface to *The Principles of Mathematics*: logicism asserts that

> . . . all pure mathematics deals exclusively with concepts definable in terms of a very small number of fundamental logical concepts, and that all its propositions are deducible from a very small number of fundamental logical principles (xv).[3]

We can characterize these parts of the thesis as the principles of *definability* and *derivability*, respectively.

1. N. Bourbaki, *Théorie des Ensembles* (Paris: Hermann, 1954), p. 4.

2. See Bertrand Russell, *Principles of Mathematics* (New York: Norton, 1903), p. 8; "Logical Atomism," in Robert C. Marsh, ed., *Logic and Knowledge* (New York: Putnam's, 1956): 321–344, pp. 325–6.

3. See also, for example, Rudolf Carnap, "The Logicist Foundations of Mathematics," in Paul Benacerraf and Hilary Putnam, eds., *Philosophy of Mathematics* (Englewood Cliffs, N.J.: Prentice-Hall, 1964) 31–41, p. 31; Carl G. Hempel, "On the Nature of Mathematical Truth," in Benacerraf and Putnam: 366–381, pp. 366ff.; J. L. Pollock, "On Logicism," in E. D. Klemke, ed., *Essays on Bertrand Russell* (Urbana: University of Illinois Press, 1970): 388–395, pp. 388–9.

The task of defining the expressions of mathematics in purely logical terms has both a syntactic and a semantic aspect. Syntactically, the claim that mathematical expressions can be defined in terms of strictly logical expressions amounts to the claim that those expressions which are characteristically mathematical can be unambiguously eliminated in favor of purely logical terms. Russell argues that a definition is merely a symbolic convention, being neither true nor false, since it is concerned only with symbols, not with what they symbolize. From a theoretical point of view, in consequence, definitions are unnecessary; they are typographical conveniences with which we can dispense, in principle if not in practice.[4] But if all definitions are superfluous in this sense and if all mathematical expressions can be defined in logical terms, then it should be possible to dispense with all mathematical expressions in favor of logical ones. The first thesis of logicism is thus that mathematics can be translated, in principle, into logic.

We can readily unpack the significance of "in principle" here; the elimination of all mathematical terms at once would lead to formulas that would be monstrously long and unreadable. It is enough that each such term can be eliminated in such a way that the translation of compounds of symbols may proceed without any ambiguity. As Kurt Gödel indicates, Russell did not achieve this aim; with more sophisticated logical techniques than were available to him, however, the achievement of unambiguous eliminability presents no deep problems.[5]

Semantically, a definition may be nothing more than a notational device holding little or no interest, but it may also have considerable significance. When engaged in the definition of some new concept, we have total freedom except for the formal requirements of unambiguous eliminability, noncreativity, etc. But in most cases that present philosophically interesting examples of analysis we are trying to define a *familiar* concept. Here the choice of symbols is not arbitrary, but rather designed to elucidate the more familiar concept; Russell mentions his definitions of cardinal and ordinal numbers and even of mathematics itself as instances of

4. Bertrand Russell and Alfred North Whitehead, *Principia Mathematica to *56* (New York: Cambridge, 1962), p. 11.

5. See "Russell's Mathematical Logic," in Benacerraf and Putnam: 211–232, p. 214.

this kind of definition.[6] It is clear from these cases that Russell thought of reduction as a relation between two interpreted theories. He concerns himself with the "ordinary employment of the term," not merely with capturing the abstract structure of a formal symbolism. Now this does not mean that the definiens and the definiendum must have the same meaning, however we are to explain *that*; Russell intends that philosophical analysis should make precise and clear what in the ordinary usage of the expression may be quite vague.

The question naturally arises, then: If "sameness of meaning" is not the criterion of adequacy for such definitions, what is? Recall that, according to Russell, definitions are not true or false; presumably, however, when we intend them as an analysis of an ordinary or previously familiar concept, we may judge them as adequate or inadequate. The criterion for such a judgment seems to be preservation of truth value: Russell praises Frege's definition of 'cardinal number' because it "leaves unchanged the truth values of all propositions in which cardinal numbers occur."[7] But Russell had in mind the preservation of truth values not just within the theory in question, but in applied or "mixed" contexts as well. Thus, it is not enough that a definition of 'three' in logical terms preserve truth values in the translation between arithmetic and set theory; it must also preserve truth values in more practical contexts, in particular, in contexts such as 'There are three *F*'s'. Russell apparently thought that this necessity singled out his as the proper explication of number; for in treating numbers as classes (or properties) of classes, it fits such contexts quite naturally and preserves the general Fregean model of predication. After all, any progression will fulfill Peano's postulates; it is the fact that interpreted theories are involved which allows Russell to prefer one of these progressions (because it conforms best to the "customary meaning"), and it is the consideration of extratheoretical contexts which singles out what Russell takes to be the

---

6. *Principles of Mathematics*, p. 3; *Principia Mathematica to *56*, pp. 11–12.

7. "Logical Atomism," p. 327. See Benacerraf, *Logicism: Some Considerations* (Ph.D. dissertation, Princeton University, 1960), pp. 2, 4; also W. V. Quine, "Truth by Convention," in *The Ways of Paradox and Other Essays* (Cambridge, Mass.: Harvard University Press, 1976): 77–106, pp. 79–80.

adequate progression and, correspondingly, the adequate set of definitions.[8]

Quine has argued quite convincingly that this represents no additional requirement and does not allow us to pick out some progression as the correct one, because counting contexts may be handled easily given any progression that fulfills the Peano axioms, together with enough of the elementary theory of relations to express the notion of a one-to-one correspondence. On his view, 'There are three F's' can be construed simply as 'The F's can be put in one-to-one correspondence with the natural numbers up to 3'. Thus if we have enough logical machinery to express the notion of a one-to-one correspondence, any progression at all will serve, practically as well as theoretically. A detailed analysis of this point must wait until chapter five, when questions concerning uniqueness will come to the fore; for now, however, we may note that Quine denies not that we must consider extratheoretical or "mixed" contexts in evaluating truth-value preservation, but only that we need anything above the concept of a one-to-one correspondence to handle them. In short, Quine does not deny that mixed contexts must be examined, but claims that in this instance they do not pose much of a difficulty and, thus, that they fail to do what Russell had planned for them.[9]

The second thesis of logicism, that all mathematical propositions may be deduced from logic, is obviously not so distinct from the first thesis as we might have supposed originally. The translations of true mathematical sentences should be true logical sentences, for the criterion of adequacy is preservation of truth value. But in this case, the mathematical propositions ought to follow from the logical propositions taken together with the required definitions.

Though the principles of definability and derivability thus blend together somewhat, the matter is somewhat more complicated than this picture suggests. Russell speaks informally of mathematics *following from* logic, but it is clear from his more careful statements and from *Principia Mathe-*

8. *Principles of Mathematics*, p. vi; see also *Introduction to Mathematical Philosophy* (London: George Allen & Unwin, 1919), pp. 8–9.

9. See Quine, *Word and Object* (Cambridge, Mass.: MIT Press, 1960), pp. 262–3; "Ontological Reduction and the World of Numbers," in *The Ways of Paradox and Other Essays*: 212–220, pp. 213–4; "Ontological Relativity," in *Ontological Relativity and Other Essays* (New York: Columbia, 1969): 26–68, pp. 44–5.

matica that he had in mind not semantic entailment but formal derivation. Of course, for Russell the distinction between these would not have seemed terribly significant, because he had no reason to believe that he had not in fact axiomatized set theory. Russell and Whitehead never asked themselves whether all mathematical truths were derivable in the *Principia* formalism; but the answer, as Gödel showed, is negative. Thus, if we take the second logicist thesis as asserting that every true mathematical proposition can be derived within a formal system employing only set-theoretic expressions and definitions of mathematical expressions in terms of them, the thesis is simply false.

As a result, if we are to save anything from the derivability thesis, we must give up either the claim that *all* the theorems of mathematics are deducible from logic or the claim that the deducibility of mathematics from logic is derivability within a formal system. Benacerraf responds to this dilemma by surrendering the former claim, requiring only that the "principle results" of mathematics be so derivable (8–10). Unfortunately for this approach, we are concerned with the reduction of mathematical *truth* to logical or set-theoretic truth; it is far from clear that a relationship of formal derivability, once we give up the claim to its universality or completeness with respect to truth, establishes the reduction of mathematical truth. It may reduce mathematical theoremhood to set-theoretic theoremhood, but even then it does so only in a restricted sense: mathematical theoremhood in a formal system S may be found to reduce to set-theoretic theoremhood in the axiomatic system S′, but which truths in each discipline are theorems of a formal system depends upon which particular formalizations we consider. Philosophically, this seems an unsatisfactory situation. The alternative, of course, is to surrender the claim that we ought to interpret deducibility as derivability in a formal system. The consequence of this move is that the two logicist theses blend further together. Mathematical truths, when we eliminate the characteristically mathematical expressions in them in favor of the logical definientia of these expressions, become logical truths; mathematical truths are thus entailed by logical truths together with the definitions. This may be more vague than the original logicist second thesis, but it has the virtue of not being obviously false. It also seems at least as clear as Benacerraf's suggestion that we pick our certain (which?) mathematical truths as "principle" ones. Perhaps, on this approach, definitional adequacy and the adequacy of the over-all reduction "hopelessly merge together" (Benacerraf, 4), but they do not become unified completely; there are still the extratheoretical contexts that are relevant to definitional adequacy but not to the deduction of mathematical truths from logical ones.

2. The Philosophy of Logical Atomism

Though Russell's motivation for the logicist project is essentially epistemological, he spends little time explaining the ontological or epistemological implications of the program, at least until the 1918 lectures on "The Philosophy of Logical Atomism." Many of the philosophical ideas presented in those lectures do not pertain to the purposes at hand, and so the portrait that follows is extremely focused: a blow-up, one might say, of those elements of logical atomism pertaining to ontological reduction.

We may view logical atomism as a generalization of the methodology of logicism to philosophical problems and theories in general; Russell, in the 1918 lectures, thinks of logicism as a paradigm of the sort of philosophical analysis that the philosophy of logical atomism recommends. Indeed, the lectures speak of logical atomism and philosophical analysis as if they were identical. Russell characterizes his view as "the view that you can get down in theory, if not in practice, to ultimate simples, out of which the world is built, and that those simples have a kind of reality not belonging to anything else."[10] Russell's program of analysis is thus in the tradition of the British empiricists, who were concerned with breaking down the complexes of experience into ultimately simple ideas, and of the rationalists as well, who attempted to recognize the foundations of knowledge in self-evident propositions and corresponding direct, unanalyzable acts of apprehension. But, for Russell, the ultimate simples to be sought are not psychological, epistemological, or phenomenal; they are *logical* simples. The complexes formed from these are logical complexes, built from the simples as advanced mathematical concepts are constructed out of expressions of set theory in *Principia*. In a few words which would provide the motto for Carnap's constructionalism, Russell formulates the central slogan of logical atomism as a philosophical method: "Wherever possible, substitute constructions out of known entities for inferences to unknown

10. "The Philosophy of Logical Atomism," in Marsh *op. cit.*: 175–282, p. 270.

entities" (326). The logical complexes that are the logical constructions out of the simples of which the world is built Russell calls "logical fictions," not because they are, as constructions, fictitious (for surely Russell would be the last person to encourage the proliferation of nondenoting terms!), but because one need not be committed to their existence as ultimate features of reality. Numbers, for example, are logical fictions, because they are classes of classes; similarly, classes are logical fictions because they can be reduced to propositional functions, or as Quine interprets it, to attributes, by way, at first, of Russell's "no-class" theory, and finally of his definition of classes in *Principia*. As a result, according to Russell, "you do not have, as part of the ultimate constituents of your world, these queer entities that you are enclined to call numbers" (270). This conclusion seems to misrepresent his more careful attitude that the establishment of something as a logical fiction does not demonstrate its nonexistence; it only indicates that we do not need to affirm its existence, in the ultimate and philosophically interesting sense with which Russell is concerned. He points out, for example: "I want to make clear that I am not *denying* the existence of anything; I am only refusing to affirm it" (273). This seems to be the moral Russell draws from the *Principia* theory of classes, concerning the existence of sets; the reducibility of classes to propositional functions shows only that we may be agnostics concerning the ultimate existence of sets. We may say with Laplace, "*Je n'ai pas besoin de cette hypothèse.*"[11]

What Russell means by 'reality', or by 'ultimate existence', is this: reality is that which must be mentioned in a complete description of the world.[12] For example, we do not have to mention numbers in such a description, since they can be eliminated in favor of sets. And sets do not have to be mentioned either, for we may eliminate them in favor of propositional functions. Russell's attitude toward the ontological status of classes, however, remains somewhat ambiguous. Though he generally seems to hold that his construction of classes justifies agnosticism with respect to them, he sometimes speaks more strongly, calling them "mere conveniences, not genuine objects," "false abstractions," and placing them in a category with "the present King of France."[13] But

11. Russell, *Introduction to Mathematical Philosophy*, p. 184.

12. "The Philosophy of Logical Atomism," p. 224; this is, of course, part of a much longer story.

13. See *Principia Mathematica to* *56, p. 72; "On the Substitutional

his willingness to commit himself more strongly to the nonexistence of classes seems to stem from the set-theoretic paradoxes. These, he argues, result from a violation of the vicious-circle principle, and that principle "requires that classes not be possible values of unrestricted variables, i.e., requires that there be no classes."[14] In general, all that the eliminability of reference to entities of a certain kind demonstrates is that one is not forced to be committed to anything of that kind as basic.

It is worth noting that Russell would later express doubts about drawing ontological conclusions from the eliminability of certain expressions; he apparently came to feel that the success of a logical construction demonstrated something quite independent of ontology, which he phrased in terms of "minimum vocabularies." A *minimum vocabulary* is a set of expressions, say A, such that no element of A can be defined in terms of the other elements of A. We can then say that A is a minimum vocabulary of a theory T if and only if every expression in the vocabulary of T can be defined in terms of expressions in A. Since definitions are theoretically unnecessary for Russell, we can speak for theoretical purposes of any theory or science as being expressed purely in terms of its minimum vocabulary. The fundamental thesis of logicism, in these terms, is that mathematics and logic have the same minimum vocabulary.

But Russell's reasons for being reluctant to draw metaphysical conclusions are hardly conclusive. First, he argues that in general minimum vocabularies are not unique; there may be several distinct minimum vocabularies for any subject matter. Given the view that reality is everything that must be mentioned in a complete description of the world, this is upsetting. Suppose that some science has several disjoint minimum vocabularies. Then no expression *must* be employed to articulate this subject matter; nothing, it appears, must be mentioned in a complete description of some aspect of the world; but this is surely an absurd conclusion. That these worries need not disturb the philosopher interested in ontological reduction will be a major contention of later chapters. Second, he fears that it is difficult to determine, based on philosophical analysis, what is truly a definition and what

Theory of Classes and Relations," in Douglas Lackey, ed., *Essays in Analysis* (New York: Braziller, 1973): 165–189, p. 166. For some details on the *Principia* theory of classes, see *20.02, *20.03, p. 188.

14. "On 'Insolubilia', and Their Solution by Symbolic Logic," in Lackey: 190–214, p. 210.

is in fact an empirical proposition. Russell's troubles concerning the analytic/synthetic distinction here apparently reflect an assumption that a definition must not be empirical if it is to carry any metaphysical weight. But this is a dubious position, since many of the reductions that have been considered successful in science have employed empirically based propositions in this role. Ernest Nagel has even regarded this sort of empirical grounding for a proposed definition as a requirement for any successful reduction. In any event, if we limit our concern to mathematical or otherwise nonempirical theories, we have little reason to worry.[15]

The position adopted by Russell in the lectures of 1918 does little to develop the formal picture of reduction beyond what was implicit in *Principia Mathematica* and some of the earlier works, but it does further develop the metaphysical significance of that picture. It is intriguing to note the influence of Ludwig Wittgenstein in the development of Russell's thinking: the view that philosophical problems tend to arise from avoidable uses of language was latent in even the theory of descriptions, but not until the logical-atomism lectures did it become explicit and become extended to questions of ontology in general.

3. Constructionalism

Rudolf Carnap's *Der Logische Aufbau der Welt (The Logical Structure of the World)* remains a brilliant example of Russellian analysis in practice. Indeed, Carnap's account of reduction is probably the clearest and most detailed to emerge from the early stages of the analytic movement. That it is a Russellian program, in outline at least, is no secret: Carnap assigns as a motto to the work Russell's maxim, "Wherever possible, substitute constructions out of known entities for inferences to unknown entities." And though Carnap reflects more than Russell does on the concept of reduction and its ontological significance, the portrait that emanates from the pages of the *Aufbau* differs little from Russell's program of analysis manifested in *Principia*.

Carnap takes as fundamental Russell's paradigm of reduction as translation: "an object is said to be 'reducible' to others, if all statements about it can be translated into state-

15. Russell, "My Mental Development," in Paul A. Schilpp, ed., *The Philosophy of Bertrand Russell* (Evanston, Ill.: The Library of Living Philosophers, v, 1946), pp. 14–16, discusses the concept of a minimum vocabulary.

ments which speak only about these other objects."[16] The construction of an object out of other objects amounts to the giving of a rule that indicates how a statement about the constructed object can be translated into statements about only the previously given objects. In more technical language, this amounts to giving a constructional definition. The definition must allow for the unambiguous elimination of the constructed object's name or description, in favor of expressions referring to those objects out of which the constructed object is created. A constructional system is an ordering of objects; those on the lowest "level," so to speak, are employed in the construction of those of the next higher level, and, in general, the objects on any level other than the lowest are constructed out of objects occurring on lower levels of the system. The objects on the lowest level are termed the *basic* objects of the system, and together they constitute the *basis* of the constructional system (6, 60–1, 65).

Two additional preliminary points are worthy of mention. First, an object that is reducible to or constructible from other objects Carnap calls a *logical complex* of these objects, which he in turn calls its *elements*. Second, reducibility is a transitive relation. Thus every object in a constructional system is a complex of the basic elements of the system (6, 61, 79). A constructional system, therefore, introduces a quasi-ordering of the objects of the system which is based upon their reducibility relations.

What, for Carnap, is the nature of a constructional definition, by means of which an object of the system is constructed? We have noticed that it must fulfill the Russellian functions of providing a translation, and thus, of allowing for the elimination of reference to the object in question. But Carnap draws a distinction between explicit definitions and definitions in use, based on Russell's distinction between explicit and contextual definitions. Explicit definitions explain the new symbols themselves, in isolation, whereas contextual definitions assign no meaning to the new symbol alone, but indicate only what it contributes to sentences containing it. To illustrate the significance of this, suppose that we are engaged in constructing an object on level one of a constructional system, where level zero is the basis of the

16. Rudolf Carnap, *The Logical Structure of the World*, Rolf George, trans. (Berkeley: University of California Press, 1967), p. 60. Parenthetical page references to Carnap will be to this book, unless otherwise noted.

system. All the expressions to be found on level zero, let us assume, are clearly designating. If we introduce any new expression by way of an explicit constructional definition, clearly this expression too will be designating. But if we introduce an expression through a definition in use, it is no longer obvious that it designates; in fact, as Carnap observes, there will be no symbol or combination of symbols constituting an equivalent of the new expression. Nevertheless, the new locution will be eliminable, but only in context. An object that is thus introduced Carnap calls a *quasi-object*. The point here is very closely related to that of Russell's theory of descriptions; the expression 'the present King of France' is an incomplete symbol which does not denote. Its meaning can be explained only by indicating how sentences containing the expression are to be translated. In Carnap's terminology, the present King of France is a quasi-object (65–67).

What is the criterion for adequacy of a constructional definition? Recall that Russell requires preservation of truth value; Carnap's criterion is virtually identical with this. Carnap distinguishes a logical from a sense translation: a logical translation preserves truth value, whereas a sense translation preserves meaning, or, in other words, the psychological and epistemic value of the sentence. A constructional transformation, according to Carnap, is a logical, but not necessarily a sense translation. A logical translation leaves the truth value of a sentence, and, correspondingly, the extension of a propositional function, unchanged. To include both of these notions, Carnap says that a constructional definition preserves *logical value*. Since this is an extensional notion, it is clear that constructional definitions need not express essential or necessary relationships (or *Begriffserklärungen*) but need only seek an "infallible and always present indicator," i.e., an expression such that the (universalized) biconditional between it and the definiendum comes out true (79–80, 83–85, 91–2, 251). Later, Carnap changed his mind on this point, deciding that the coextensiveness of the two terms of a definition must be necessary, based on logical rules or natural laws; he also gave up the claim that such definitions are always possible, allowing that a constructional system might proceed with more liberal forms of concept building (viii, ix).

So far we have discussed the ordering that a constructional system introduces among the objects of the system as if it were uniquely determined by the reducibility relations holding among those objects. But Carnap recognizes that often this is not the case: "Frequently, these relations hold in different directions, so that they alone do not uniquely determine the order of the system."[17] In such cases, the structure of the system is based not only upon those relations but upon epistemic primacy. The theory of construction thus becomes the whole of what Carnap takes to be the legitimate theory of knowledge, i.e., epistemology (88–9, 94, 286). The theme of the relationship between epistemic primacy and the ordering of reducibility relations will become crucially important in chapters seven and eight, so a detailed discussion of Carnap's notion will be delayed until then.

Clearly the outlines of Carnap's treatment of reduction bear similarity to the account developed but not explicitly argued for, to any such extent, by Russell. These accounts lack precision in their formulation, and, to be sure, they differ in some respects. But perhaps the most important difference is not in the paradigm itself, but in the relation between the account of reduction *per se* and questions of ontology. As we noted, for Russell the reducibility of an object liberates us from commitment to its ultimate existence; for Carnap, however, questions of "ultimate existence" do not make sense. Carnap's distinction between empirical reality and metaphysical reality comes into play here; for only empirical reality (and questions such as Is there a town called Punxsutawney in Pennsylvania? or Is there a prime number between the squares of ten and eleven?) has any place within a constructional system (95, 273, 282–3). Questions of metaphysical reality are questions of traditional ontology (Are there *really* towns, or just configurations of individuals? or Are there *really* numbers?) which Carnap eschews. Russell, of course, was willing to contemplate such questions, and certainly considered them meaningful, at least in his earlier stages. The philosophy of logical atomism was based on the supposition that there are ultimate simples, which alone possess precisely what Carnap has in mind by metaphysical reality. At times Carnap speaks as if this concept, though perhaps legitimate, does not fall into the realm of constructional theory (88). But the nonscientific character of questions of metaphysical reality implies their nonrationality and, thus, eventually their meaninglessness. Ontological theses are not even false: "the question of their truth of falsity cannot even

---

17. *The Logical Structure of the World*, p. 88; interreducibility, or what I shall call "mutual reducibility," holds between some very important domains of objects, for example, the physical and the psychological; see p. 92.

be posed."[18] Perhaps this view accounts for Carnap's insistence on speaking of correlations, rather than identities, with regard to the logicist construction of mathematics.[19]

This discussion of constructionalism cannot be complete without a consideration of Nelson Goodman's *The Structure of Appearance*, which sets forth a constructional system in the tradition of Carnap and which devotes considerable energy to the discussion of the notion of a constructional system in general. I have been urging that an examination of the work of Russell and Carnap reveals a fairly unified concept of reduction; Goodman, however, challenges the Russell-Carnap paradigm in an important way. Goodman's chief concern is the Russell-Carnap criterion of definitional adequacy or, in Goodman's terms, accuracy. Recall that both Russell and Carnap hold that a definition is accurate for the purposes of reduction if it satisfies the condition of preservation of truth value; this comes to a requirement of extensional identity, for if the definition is of a propositional function, it is accurate if and only if the definiens and the definiendum have identical extensions. The test of this would appear to be substitutability *salva veritate* within extensional contexts.

Goodman finds a number of problems with this general account of definitional accuracy:

(1) If we simple-mindedly go about replacing all the occurrences of the definiendum with the definiens, we are bound to violate the requirement of truth-value preservation, even with definitions that might otherwise seem perfectly acceptable. Extratheoretical examples provide good instances of this phenomenon: 'The Pirates won five more games than the Reds' becomes 'The Pirates won $\{\{\{\{\{\phi\}\}\}\}\}$ more games than the Reds', perhaps, and 'There is one F', in general, becomes something like 'There is $\{\phi\}$ F'. Neither of these transliterations makes particularly good sense. We might think that such sentences matter little, and so try to come up with some way of excluding them from consideration. But some sentences that give analogous troubles must be dealt with: consider '1 is less than 2', which, under the substitutability test, comes out as '$\{\phi\}$ is less than 2'; '$\{\phi\}$ is prime', '$\{\phi\}$ is a factor of 8', etc., fare no better. We are not likely to

18. "Pseudoproblems in Philosophy," in *The Logical Structure of the World*, p. 334.

19. "The Logicist Foundations of Mathematics," p. 33. For more on the distinction between correlations and assertions of identity, see chapters five and six.

consider such sentences true, or even well formed. The problem here, at least in part, is that the other terms in these sentences are not being replaced by their systematic counterparts. So the criterion, if it is to be workable, must shift to deal with the translation of sentences rather than the substitutability of terms. Surely this is what Russell, at least, had in mind from the beginning.

(2) Once we convert the test to one that relates to sentences and their truth values under transformations by way of constructional definitions, we must be prepared, it seems, to test any sentence relating any two terms of the theory whatever. But this has as a consequence that we cannot test any constructional definition until we have developed a complete definitional system. Now this difficulty might be resolved by insisting that only sentences that can be fully translated into the system retain their truth values. After all, in evaluating the success of the Russell-Whitehead definitions of numbers, we are unlikely to be concerned with the preservation of the truth value of a sentence such as 'Lady Amberley was a radical', but will be concerned only with those sentences which are capable of being translated fully into the *Principia* reductive schema.

(3) There are generally many ways of reducing one theory to another, or one set of objects to another. But frequently the terms that constitute possible definientia of the terms of the reduced theory are not themselves extensionally equivalent with one another. A blatant example of this is the reduction of arithmetic to set theory, which will occupy a large portion of succeeding chapters. Say that, on different constructions of arithmetic, we identify the number 2 with two different sets, in the one case $\{\{\phi\}\}$, and in the other $\{\phi, \{\phi\}\}$. It is obvious that these sets are not identical with each other. Though this directly concerns not extensional identity but identity itself, the point is the same: we may consider identity the limiting case of the problem of extensional identity of predicates, since we may construe '$=\{\{\phi\}\}$' as a predicate true of one and only one object. Thus, whenever we face multiple possible constructions, the criterion of extensional identity becomes problematic.

(4) A final problem relates once again to the possibility of a multiplicity of reductions between the same sets of concepts. Suppose we are dealing with a system that translates the number 2 into $\{\phi, \{\phi\}\}$, and we are concerned with the sentence from another possible reduction, '$2 = \{\{\phi\}\}$'. This translates into the rubric as '$\{\phi, \{\phi\}\} = \{\{\phi\}\}$', which is

plainly false. The criterion does not allow us sufficient flexibility to cover such troublesome sentences. It is enough, it might seem, that a translation be truth-value preserving with respect to those sentences which we care about; but, as Goodman indicates, this is not so much a criterion as a criterion of criteria.[20]

Goodman admits that there may be a number of ways out of the labyrinth that these objections have created. One possibility is to specify that the class of sentences we must be concerned with is really a very restricted class, e.g., the sentences within some formalized theory. This may reflect Carnap's general intentions, and it harmonizes with a Wittgensteinian approach to the matter: we need concern ourselves only with the sentences of the science at hand, and the constructional definitions may be considered ladders which are strictly meaningless. But if we are concerned not with the question of whether arithmetic, specified formally, reduces to set theory on a given formalization, but rather with the broader question of whether expressions that designate numbers can be eliminated from our discourse, then, as Russell insists, extratheoretical contexts must be taken into consideration. Even if formalized number theory is translatable into some other theory, we cannot achieve the ontological aims of a reduction in Russell's sense unless extratheoretical occurrences of number-theoretic discourse can be translated away as well (7–8). In any event, this option leaves untouched some of the difficulties arising from the possibility of multiple reductions.

A second option is that of claiming that constructional definitions and thus identity statements such as '$1 = \{\phi\}$' are truth-value-less outside the context of a given system. About this option I shall have much to say later on: this is essentially the strategy that chapter five adopts for dealing with problems arising from multiple reductions.

Goodman chooses to weaken the criterion of extensional identity to extensional isomorphism. What Goodman means by 'isomorphism' here differs from what the term means in most contexts; in spite of the 'iso-' prefix, for example, Goodman's concept is not symmetric. The notion of an extensional isomorphism is closely tied to the fundamentals of

---

20. Nelson Goodman, *The Structure of Appearance* (Boston: Reidel, 1951, 1977), p. 9. The discussion of the past few pages has been based on pp. 3–9. Goodman uses a geometrical rather than an arithmetical example to illustrate these difficulties. Further parenthetical page references to Goodman will be to this work, unless noted otherwise.

Goodman's nominalism, and a thorough discussion and evaluation of the criterion would require more analysis of the position than we have time to perform. It is unclear, in particular, just how much of classical mathematics can be reconstructed within Goodman's framework. But since these matters reach beyond the present topic, I shall give only a brief summary of Goodman's solution.

The necessary and sufficient condition for the accuracy of a constructional definition is that the definiens be extensionally isomorphic to the definiendum (10, 18, 20). More generally, Goodman says, "the set of all the definientia of a system must be extensionally isomorphic to the set of all the definienda" (10). That these formulations are equivalent we can see from the definition of isomorphism. "A relation R is *isomorphic* to a relation S in the sense here intended if and only if R can be obtained by consistently replacing the ultimate factors in S" (10–1). The *components* of a sequence are the elements that occupy entire places in the sequence; if we dissolve each of the components into its components (if it is itself a sequence) or into its members (if it is a class) and if we continue this process until the elements reached have no further elements or components, the factors that remain are the *ultimate factors* of the sequence. Goodman's demand of consistent replacement "requires only that each not-null ultimate factor be replaced by one and only one not-null element; that different not-null ultimate factors always be replaced by different not-null elements; and that the null class be always replaced by itself" (10–1). This sort of isomorphism is not symmetric, simply because some of the elements that replace ultimate factors in such an operation need not be ultimate factors themselves. We should think of this sort of isomorphism, then, not on the model of isomorphism between semantical structures in model theory, but rather as something like the relation that an axiom of some formalized theory bears to an axiom schema of that theory.

We can raise a number of problems concerning Goodman's criterion for definitional accuracy. First, the criterion assumes that the extensions of the terms related by the definition are precisely specified, and, as Carl Hempel has observed, this is a condition that is rarely satisfied.[21] Second, the objection that the later Carnap raises against his own earlier criterion in the *Aufbau* bears on Goodman's account as well; the cri-

---

21. "Reflections on Nelson Goodman's *The Structure of Appearance*," *Philosophical Review*, LXII (1953): 108–116, p. 113.

terion, being purely extensional, requires no necessary or lawlike connections between the defined terms. Whether this is in fact a weakness or not, it is irrelevant to the consideration of reduction with regard to theories involving ostensible commitments to abstract objects. As a philosopher who criticizes Goodman on these grounds himself points out,

> In defining mathematical concepts, however, we never rely on purely contingent properties of the objects concerned (we do not, to give a crude example, define '9' as 'the number of the planets'); all our definitions are in purely mathematical terms, and thus our definitions are always either necessarily adequate or necessarily inadequate.[22]

Third, Goodman's criterion seems to raise difficulties concerning reductions that otherwise appear perfectly acceptable from a formal point of view. Let us call elementary number theory, but with '+' as the only operation symbol, "Presburger arithmetic." This theory is easily translatable into set theory. Now take this set-theoretic translation of Presburger arithmetic (according to some translation manual or other), which we may call T, and form another theory T' by replacing the set-theoretic relation symbols by dummy letters 'F', 'G', etc., and mapping the sequence of sets representing the numbers in T into another sequence, which represents the numbers in T'. Say that 'ϕ', '$\{\phi\}$', '$\{\{\phi\}\}$', etc., represent '0', '1', '2', etc., in T; then we may construct 'ϕ', '$\{\{\phi\}\}$', '$\{\{\{\{\phi\}\}\}\}$', etc., by doubling the number of brackets around the null set in each element of the sequence in T, to obtain representatives of the numbers in T'. Let us assume, of course, that we can make the operation symbols in T' reflect this move. What is the relationship between T and T'? The difference between them appears to be specious; we have a situation analogous to that which Russell discusses, where we might alter arithmetic by letting '100' represent '0', '101' represent '1', etc. Thus we are tempted to say not only that Presburger arithmetic reduces to both T and T', but that T' reduces to T, being in fact a trivial variant of the same theory, or at least a theory with the same basic structure. Yet, on Goodman's account, T and T' cannot be reduced to each other. Goodman's definition of consistent replacement re-

---

22. Michael Dummett, "Constructionalism," *Philosophical Review*, LXVI (1957): 47–65, p. 63.

quires that the null set be everywhere replaced by itself; it is therefore impossible to transform any set of the standard cumulative hierarchy into another such set under Goodman's conception of isomorphism. So though an infinite number of sequences of sets might be taken as representative of the numbers, none of this infinite collection is isomorphic to any others. Presburger arithmetic can still reduce to a theory taking each as representative of the numbers, since isomorphism is not symmetric, but we cannot explain the relationship between these distinct set-theoretic accounts of number.

Furthermore, we might normally think that T and T', being nothing more than translations of Presburger arithmetic into set theory, ought to reduce to Presburger arithmetic. But this could be possible only if the definientia (now in Presburger arithmetic) are isomorphic to the definienda (in T or T'). Thus we should be able to obtain a given definiens in Presburger arithmetic by consistently replacing the ultimate factors in a set-theoretic definiendum. But in any such definiendum in T or T', there will be a single ultimate factor: 'ϕ'. By the definition of consistent replacement, this must always be replaced by itself. As a result, we have no way of getting from the set-theoretic fragments to Presburger arithmetic, or, for that matter, to any theory without sets in its domain. It follows that, on Goodman's account, set theory cannot be reduced to any other theory in a sense that could have any interest for ontology. Since set theory is probably the most important single theory in our conceptual scheme which involves a commitment to abstract objects, this consequence of Goodman's analysis of reduction is very damaging indeed.

We might try to revise Goodman's definition, by linking the notion of extensional isomorphism closely to his nominalism. His model for construing the set-theoretic relation 'x is an element of y' in the mereological calculus is the quasi-physical relation 'x is a part of y'. On this interpretation, two sets that contain the same ultimate factors ought to be identical, for two wholes with the same physical parts coincide.[23] Of course, this revision would make isomorphism an equivalence relation. But its application to set theory would once again be problematic. Goodman's definitions do not specify how we are to treat duplications of ultimate factors, but the account seems to imply that only the identity of the ultimate factors matters; the number of times an ultimate factor ap-

23. See Goodman and Quine, "Steps toward a Constructive Nominalism," *Journal of Symbolic Logic*, xii (1947): 105–122; Goodman, "A World of Individuals," in Benacerraf and Putnam: 197–210.

pears in the fully resolved sequence would seem to be irrelevant. But this is the only thing that might distinguish some of the sets of the standard cumulative hierarchy, formed from a base level containing only the null set, from any others.

This may not appear to be very disconcerting, since presumably any set might be used as a translation for '2', or any other number. What is upsetting, however, is that this revision of Goodman's criterion is fashioned in such a way that all the sets of the cumulative hierarchy are indistinguishable from the perspective of extensional isomorphism. Any definition of any set-theoretic notion will look like any other, whether legitimate, productive, or even coherent, or not; each will be constituted by the single ultimate factor 'ϕ'. So long as we remain within the cumulative hierarchy with the null set as the only individual, any definition will be extensionally isomorphic to any other, and any set of definitions will be isomorphic to any other. Our revision of Goodman's criterion thus offers no restriction at all on the accuracy of proposed constructional definitions.

Someone might object that the alternative definitions are sets, not relations or sequences as Goodman's definitions suppose. But this we may take care of trivially: a set may be construed as a sequence with a single component or element, and '$=\{\phi\}$', for example, may be thought of as a monadic relation. It may also be objected that the cumulative hierarchy with 'ϕ' as the only individual is a construction so utterly repulsive to the nominalist that we have no reason to expect that Goodman's criterion would apply to it unproblematically. This, however, is a mistake. First, the definitions of the relevant terms, especially that of 'consistent replacement', count the null set as a legitimate unit to be analyzed within the context of the applicability of the definitions. Furthermore, suppose that one could construct a nominalistic reduction of set theory, and thus of the cumulative hierarchy, or at least some portion of it sufficient for modeling the natural numbers and, in general, arithmetic. If the set-theoretic terms involved in this could be construed as acceptable to the nominalist, then we could have not only a reduction of that portion of set theory, but also a nominalistic reduction of arithmetic; this extension is reasonable because of the reduction of arithmetic to the reduced portion of set theory. But Goodman's account, if this objection is to be taken seriously, would have to contend that, although that portion of set theory to which arithmetic reduces is acceptable nominalistically, arithmetic cannot be considered *ipso facto* acceptable. And, in general, where T reduces to T', T' reduces to T'', and T'' is a nominalistically acceptable theory, we want to be able to say that T and T' are also acceptable, whatever their specific contents or commitments. Given our understanding of reduction, then, the consequences of altogether excluding the null set from consideration would be absurd.

One might think, then, that Goodman's conception of the ontological signficance of reduction dramatically differs from that which I have been defending. But Goodman's view is essentially Russellian — reduction for him allows the avoidance of ontological commitment, but does not entail the nonexistence or the derivative character of what is reduced — though it is more highly developed. A constructional system itself is noncommittal on ontological questions; this is not, as for Carnap, due to the nonrational nature of the issues, but rather to the nature of constructional systems. A theory about intersecting lines, for example, may be isomorphic in the relevant sense to a theory about a collection of gorillas, but in exhibiting this relationship we are not entitled to assume that the gorillas have been shown not to exist, or to exist only as constructions out of intersecting lines.[24]

Ontological commitment, for Goodman, is determined by the use of variables within a theory: "if we use variables that we construe as having entities of a given kind as values, we acknowledge that there are such entities" (24–25). This is the familiar Quinean position. The use of variables that take as values objects of a certain kind can be maintained without ontological commitment only if (1) these variables are eliminable, or (2) the language involved can be explained as merely a computational device, an "abacus" having no meaning or significance in itself.[25] The first alternative is reduction, and its foundation is the eliminability of a mode of discourse, which is a characteristically Russellian theme. Now it seems obvious that given a set-theoretic model of arithmetic in terms of the standard cumulative hierarchy, the language of arithmetic is indeed in principle eliminable. We can replace it with the language of sets; if this can be construed as nominalistically acceptable, then, the nominalist need not be troubled about the commitments of arithmetic.

According to Goodman, the result of these views for ontol-

---

24. The example is Goodman's. See *The Structure of Appearance*, pp. 20–1.

25. Goodman, p. 25; see Goodman and Quine, p. 122.

ogy is that "the reductive force of a constructional system consists not in showing that a given entity is identical with a complex of other entities but in showing that no commitment to the contrary is necessary" (21–22). It is intriguing to note that Goodman looks to epistemology for inspiration concerning the nature of the constructional system to be established, since there are no absolute primitives and since there are many possible and accurate definitions of most of the required concepts. This epistemological significance of constructional systems we have seen to be characteristic of Russell and Carnap as well, and will later emerge as a crucial insight into the nature of reduction as a philosophical activity.

4. *Formalization*

I shall close this chapter with an attempt to formalize, at least roughly, the conception of reduction which has emerged from our examination of the views of Russell, Carnap, and Goodman. I have argued that a unified notion pervades their work, which can be sharpened to provide a viable account of ontological reduction for theories involving ostensible commitments to abstract entities. I shall begin, therefore, by taking seriously Russell's statement that mathematics follows from logic. This is the essence of the derivational paradigm of reduction which Russell advances; how can we formalize the idea of one theory's following from another?

Let us begin by assuming that one theory, *M*, follows from another theory, *L*. Now we have no clear idea of what it is for one *theory* to follow logically from something; the notion must be derivative, based upon the concept of a sentence or formula following from a set of premises. The set of premises we may take initially as *L*. To say that *M* follows from *L* we might say that each formula or statement of *M* follows from *L*. Furthermore, if we construe a theory as a set of sentences closed under logical consequence, this amounts to saying that each formula in *M* is also in *L*: that, in other words, *M* is a subset of *L*. In this sense, then, we could say that *M* follows from *L* just in case *M* is a subtheory of *L*.

Russell does not mean, however, to present such a simple concept of reduction. After all, mathematics and logic have different vocabularies; each mathematical theorem does not follow from logic in the sense of already being a logical truth. Recall that the thesis of logicism is, in the beginning, twofold: mathematical concepts can be defined in terms of logical concepts, and, given those definitions, mathematical truths follow from logical truths. Thus we need not require that M follow from L immediately; M must follow from L, taken together with the set of definitions (call it D) linking the terms of M and L in accordance with the principle of definability. By applying the above reasoning, then, M must be a subtheory of $L \cup D$. But how can we characterize the set of definitions D?

We want, Russell would say, a definition of every characteristically mathematical expression in terms of purely logical expressions. This is guaranteed if we have a definition of every primitive predicate of M in terms of the vocabulary of L, for then the definition of more complex definable expressions can proceed recursively by breaking each complex into its component primitives. (We may assume that we have eliminated singular terms from the language, for the sake of simplicity; they will be easy to build in later.) Imagine $V(M)$, then, as the set of primitive predicates of M, $V^*(M)$ as the set of predicative expressions of M, and $V^*(L)$ as the set of predicative expressions available in L. We want definitions that will link each term in $V(M)$ to some element of $V^*(L)$, thus connecting each element of $V^*(M)$ to an element of $V^*(L)$ as well. (We assume that $V(M)$ and $V^*(M)$ can be so connected, for otherwise the elements of $V(M)$ would not count as the *primitive* predicates of M.) For Russell and the early Carnap, these definitions will be (universalized) biconditionals. Thus we construct a set of formulas, with one and only one element for each element of $V(M)$, having the form

$$(x_1, \ldots, x_n) \, (F(x_1, \ldots, x_n) \equiv A(x_1, \ldots, x_n))$$

where F is an n-ary primitive predicate of M [i.e., an element of $V(M)$] and A is an expression with n free variables in L [i.e., an element of $V^*(L)$]. It appears, then, that we may say that M follows from L just in case there is such a set of definitions D, such that M is a subtheory of $L \cup D$.

Russell and Carnap, however, frequently talk of reduction as involving translation; Goodman similarly speaks of constructional transformations. Our account so far does not explain this terminology. To accomplish that, we may transfer, as it were, the definitions of the terms of M into the metalanguage. Thus we can construct a function t that takes as arguments the predicates of M and takes as values the expressions of L, which preserves -ariness, i.e., which carries each n-ary predicate into a formula with n free variables. The translation function t thus transforms the statements of M into statements of L. But how do we know that the translation has any philosophical signficance? Russell's answer is that it must preserve truth value; Carnap responds that the function must preserve logical value. What do we need, however, to ensure that M follows from L? Clearly, the transformations of the theorems of M must be theorems of L. Thus we may say, minimally, that the translations must be theorem-preserving. We have, then, a function t from $V(M)$ into $V^*(L)$ such that, if A is a theorem of M, the transformation of A under t (i.e., the formula that results from the substitution of the definitions of the primitive predicates in A for those predicates, throughout the formula) is a theorem of L. Speaking once again of theories as logically closed sets of sentences, we may say that, if A is an element of M, the transformation of A under t is an element of L. Thus from the theory M we construct M', the set of the transformations of the theorems of M under t, such that M' is a subtheory of L.

The formalization of the derivational concept of reduction still retains a number of rough edges. What is the relationship between truth-value preservation and theorem preservation? How do we go about specifying the theories under consideration? How do we go about translating complex predicates? What are the formal properties of these characterizations of reduction? What are the characteristics of D? In particular, how do we single out one such set, if more than one is available? These are important questions which deserve to be answered. Doing them justice will be a substantial concern of the chapters to come.

3 Intertheoretic Explanation

In this chapter I shall look to philosophers who have attempted to explain the reduction of one scientific theory to another for inspiration in our search for an adequate account of ontological reduction. In spite of Lawrence Sklar's warning that "whatever is meant by the claim that arithmetic is reducible to logic, or more conservatively to set theory, it is not that arithmetic is related to the more fundamental theory in anything like the way in which a physical theory is related to a theory to which it reduces,"[1] we shall find scientific reductions quite instructive, even though we are concerned with theories ostensibly committing us to abstract entities. Scientific theories, after all, generally include a substantial amount of mathematics. Thus physical theories frequently carry very significant commitments to abstract objects: to mathematical entities as well as to characteristically physical entities such as paths or forces. We might expect, then, that any adequate account of reduction in science would include an account of reduction with regard to abstract entities. We shall find, in fact, that when their strictly empirical elements are removed, accounts of scientific reduction either present an account very close to the derivational account advanced by Russell and Carnap or fail to apply to problems involving abstract entities altogether.

1. The Derivational Model

I shall turn to four distinct models of reduction considered as a scientific activity and analyze their implications for reductions involving abstract objects. Reduction in the empirical sciences has most often been considered a sort of intertheoretic explanation; when one theory reduces to another, it is explained by that reducing theory. Thus if statistical mechanics reduces classical thermodynamics, the behavior of large-scale masses (e.g., gases) is explained by the account of the behavior of small-scale masses provided by statistical mechanics. If we combine this view with the traditional Hempel-Oppenheim covering-law account of scientific ex-

---

1. "Types of Intertheoretic Reduction," *British Journal for the Philosophy of Science*, XVIII (1967): 109–124, p. 109. Parenthetical page references to Sklar will be to this paper, unless otherwise noted.

planation, the result is the derivational model of reduction in science.

Ernest Nagel deserves the credit for developing the derivational model of intertheoretic explanation. He distinguishes between homogeneous and heterogeneous reductions, but the former merit little interest, since the theories involved employ the same vocabulary. With respect to heterogeneous reductions, Nagel specifies two necessary conditions for reduction: the condition of connectability and the condition of derivability. Where 'A' is a term absent from the theoretical vocabulary of the reducing science, the condition of connectability states that "assumptions of some kind must be introduced which postulate suitable relations between whatever is signified by 'A' and traits represented by theoretical terms already present in the primary science."[2] The condition of derivability requires that "with the help of these additional assumptions, all the laws of the secondary science, including those containing the term 'A', must be logically derivable from the theoretical premises and their associated coordinating definitions in the primary discipline" (353–54).

Before considering these requirements in more detail, we may ask about their interrelation. After all, though Russell characterizes logicism as consisting of two theses, we have found that these theses are not distinguished very clearly. The condition of derivability, according to Nagel, implies the condition of connectability, and is stated separately only for heuristic value (355n). A term that has not appeared in the premises of the deductive explanation of a reduced law can appear in that law only vacuously, that is, in such a way that any other term could be substituted for it without affecting the validity of the deduction. This is an uninteresting case, of course, so it does seem that nonvacuous derivability entails connectability.

But does the condition of connectability entail the condition of derivability? This logical relationship is more problematic. Kemeny and Oppenheim argue that if the connecting assumptions are biconditionals this implication holds. Nagel admits that this is correct, but is unwilling to grant that for every term appearing in the reduced but not in the reducing science there is a term of the reducing science linked to it

2. *The Structure of Science* (New York: Harcourt, Brace & World, 1961; Indianapolis: Hackett Publishing Company, 1979), pp. 353–4. References to Nagel will be to this book, unless otherwise noted.

by a biconditional.[3] We may clarify the point by recalling again Russell's account of reduction: the two logicist theses pertain to the definability of concepts and the derivability of truths. If the definability condition is fulfilled, there is a translation from the theory to be reduced into the reducing theory; so long as this translation is truth-preserving, then, the derivability itself is assured. But this happens only because the criterion of definitional adequacy is truth-value preservation. Nagel's account offers us a different criterion of definitional adequacy; so the conclusion does not follow, even if all the linking laws are biconditionals. We might be able to find a set of linking biconditionals which would allow for the translation of the laws to be reduced, but which transformed them into statements that were false by the laws of the reducing theory. On Nagel's account the linking laws must be "well-supported", but this does not appear to guarantee preservation of truth value. Thus connectability does not imply derivability.

This brings us to the question of the status of the connecting assumptions on Nagel's account of scientific reduction. He considers three alternatives: that they are logical links; that they are conventional; and that they are factual connections. That they are entirely connections of meaning or of convention he rules out immediately, for that would imply that reduction can be achieved without any empirical investigation. In essence, therefore, the connecting assumptions are factual in character; they require evidential support for their justification and acceptance.

Nagel realizes that it is not safe to pretend that connecting assumptions can be categorized so neatly, in a post-Quine environment, and he admits that the "cognitive status" of the linking laws depends on the context in which they are used. On one formulation of the reduction of one science to another, a given law may be treated as conventional or definitional, while on another formulation of the same reductive relationship, we may think of the law as factual (356–7).

In any event, Nagel commits himself to the extensional character of the assumptions connecting the terms of the two theories. Whether there is anything more than this involved

3. See John Kemeny and Paul Oppenheim, "On Reduction", *Philosophical Studies*, VII (1956): 6–19, p. 10; Nagel, p. 355n.; for a criticism of the Kemeny-Oppenheim argument, see J. W. Swanson, "On the Kemeny-Oppenheim Treatment of Reduction," *Philosophical Studies*, XIII (1962): 94–96.

or not, at least we may conclude that the bridge laws are empirical hypotheses concerning the extensions of scientific predicates.[4] They say, roughly, that two extensions are identical or that one extension is a subset of another; in other words, the laws may be expressed as universalized material conditionals or biconditionals (126).

To what extent does this account apply to the problem of reductions involving theories with ostensible commitments to abstract entities? The factual nature of the connecting assumptions has no significance in mathematics, as long as we reject a very literal platonism, with its attendant "perception" of abstract objects, which would make mathematics as empirical as any other science. Russell's view, without its accompanying platonism, pictures these relations as essentially relations of meaning, for adherence to the "customary meaning" of the term is a crucial method for deciding between alternative formally acceptable reductions. The next chapter will adopt the view that the connecting assumptions are conventional in nature when abstract objects are concerned.

We should note that, though these are necessary, formal conditions for reduction, they are not sufficient. As nonformal conditions for reduction, Nagel mentions the degree of support of the connecting laws, the fertility of the reduction for scientific theorization and research, the degree of support of the primary science, and even then confesses that a reduction may have little or no effect on knowledge if the sciences concerned are not in proper stages of development (358–362).

If we ask what Nagel takes the ontological implications of reduction in this sense to be, we find no clear answer. He holds that questions concerning the reduction of one theory to another are replacements for metaphysical questions concerning the dependence or ultimate status of entities; in keeping with the "linguistic turn" of contemporary philosophy, he focuses on syntactic and semantic questions concerning the relations of linguistic entities rather than on the ontological relations of nonlinguistic objects of various sorts. In particular, Nagel bristles at a tendency to construe issues pertaining to the methodology of research as problems relating to the "immutable structure of the universe".[5] This chal-

4. See Nagel, "Issues in the Logic of Reductive Explanations," in H. Kiefer and M. Munitz, eds., *Mind, Science, and History* (Albany: SUNY Press, 1970), pp. 126–7.

5. See *The Structure of Science*, pp. 363–4, and also Clark Glymour, "Some Patterns of Reduction," *Philosophy of Science*, XXXVII (1970): 340–353, p. 340.

lenges the project on which we have embarked, namely, the attempt to give an adequate account of ontological reduction. But Nagel's disdain for metaphysics does not indicate that the logical relationships between theories cannot have any kind of metaphysical significance. In fact, insofar as one is willing to talk about the semantical relationships between theories, one should be willing to consider the domains of the theories and their possible relationships as well.

One of the most important controversies concerning the derivational model of reduction as a scientific activity concerns the alleged role of connecting assumptions. Nagel holds that these may have the form, logically, of either conditionals or biconditionals, thus weakening the Russellian paradigm of linking definitions. Some philosophers have argued, however, that this weakening distorts the nature of reduction and that connecting laws must be at least biconditionals, perhaps even necessary biconditionals, or identities of one form or another.

Carl Hempel contends that, though conditionals suffice for the derivation of laws, they do not allow for the derivation of concepts. The conditional statements do not allow for the elimination of the secondary theory's terminology in any direct way, and so the deduction of the laws of that theory requires the employment of concepts unique to it. If T is the theory to be reduced, T' is the reducing theory, and C is the set of connecting principles, at least some of which are conditionals required for the derivation of the laws of T, then it seems that T has been reduced not to T' but to $T' \cup C$ instead. The point recalls the Russellian paradigm, for it stresses the centrality of the eliminability of the terms of the reduced theory. These terms cannot be eliminated fully without connecting biconditionals simply because some expressions will have no characterization in the terms of the reducing theory, and the appearance of these expressions in the connecting principles will be crucial to the success of the reduction.[6] Even these biconditionals are not free from difficulty; typically a reduction broadens concepts, so that the extensions of the terms are not strictly identical (189). Nevertheless, from one point of view of the logic of reduction, Hempel argues, biconditionals are essential in guaranteeing the eliminability of the reduced theory. Much the same argument has been

6. Carl G. Hempel, "Reduction: Ontological and Linguistic Facets," in Sidney Morgenbesser, Patrick Suppes, and Morton White, eds., *Philosophy, Science, and Method* (New York: St. Martin's, 1969): 179–199, pp. 188–9.

advanced by Lawrence Sklar: correlations between theories which take the form of universalized conditionals establish only the derivability of T from T' and C. This, however, falls under Nagel's "homogeneous" reduction rubric, where the reduced theory contains no term nonvacuously which is not present in the reducing theory. But the reducibility of T to $T' \cup C$ is not the same as the reducibility of T to T' (119).

Sklar and Kenneth Schaffner have argued an even stronger point: that the biconditionals linking the two theories involved should be interpreted as synthetic identities.[7] First, the interpretation of linking assumptions as identities has a clear ontological significance; Schaffner (143n) claims that "it is only by the use of synthetic identities that reduction can decrease the ontology" of the over-all conceptual scheme. Second, as Sklar observes, the treatment of linking biconditionals as mere correlations, as opposed to identities, makes no sense: "What would it be to *correlate* the piece of salt with an array of atoms at the same place and time rather than to identify the salt as an array of atoms?" (120). Third, identifications are important in that they avoid the need for explanation. Reconsider the possibility of connecting assumptions having the form of conditionals; they constitute a theory in themselves, indispensable to the reduction, which requires evidential support and explanation just as other laws of the reducing theory do. Biconditionals, however, though they avoid the technical problem, still require explanation as seeming scientific laws. Identities, on the other hand, do not require explanation: "you cannot, as many have pointed out, ask *why* light waves are electromagnetic waves" (121). Instead, identifications transfer the need for explanation to some other part of the theory, or often to some other theory altogether. This becomes important in mathematical contexts: what kind of explanation could there be for a correlation between, for example, sets and numbers? No explanations for connecting laws can be given in mathematics, except for an appeal to analogical functioning within the two theories involved. But the distinction between biconditionals and "synthetic identities" makes little sense in mathematical contexts. We might think of synthetic identities involving predicates as necessary universalized biconditionals, where the necessity is understood as synthetic rather than logical. In mathematical contexts, however, the distinction between synthetic and

7. Sklar, pp. 120–2; Kenneth Schaffner, "Approaches to Reduction," *Philosophy of Science*, XXXIV (1967): 137–147, p. 143; parenthetical page references to Schaffner will be to this article.

logical or analytic necessity seems to have no application, and the distinction between necessary and contingent statements likewise seems irrelevant. Thus, the revisions to the derivational paradigm advanced by Sklar and Schaffner, though significant in scientific contexts of a general sort, have little importance in mathematics. They fail to apply, in fact, whenever ostensible commitments to abstract objects are at issue, for the above distinctions have no more relevance to nonmathematical abstracta than to mathematical objects.

The same points, in essence, apply to Robert Causey's work on microreduction. A microreduction, intuitively, is a reduction where the objects of the reducing theory are spatial parts of the objects of the theory to be reduced. More technically, "a *microreduction* of T_2 to T_1 is a reduction of T_2 to T_1 in which the elements of Dom_2 are identified with certain elements of Dom_1."[8] Clearly the notion of a microreduction is closely linked to that of ontological reduction. Causey endorses the derivational model of reduction in science: "Obviously in a reduction of T_2 one must derive, and he needs only to derive, the fundamental laws of T_2" (200). Causey also endorses the Hempel-Sklar view that biconditional bridge laws are necessary to effect a reduction to the proper theory, rather than to an enlargement of it making essential use of the terms of the reduced theory. Finally, Causey insists that the connecting laws must be identities; his theory employs "Thing-Identity Bridge Laws", "Attribute-Identity Bridge Laws", etc. Apparently, he regards the connecting assumptions as both identities between attributes and biconditionals and considers them necessary universalized biconditionals in form, as did Schaffner and Sklar. His justification for this is twofold. First, once again, it does not make sense to speak of a mere correlation of, for instance, a water molecule with a certain H_2O structure; the two are identical. Second, identities are not subject to explanation. If the connecting assumptions were subject to explanation, they would amount to a theory in their own right, and the reduction would be not to the original theory but to an enlargement of it, containing a "theory of the relationship between T_1 and T_2". Every reduction would then be homogeneous. But, in scientific practice, we find no special linking theories

8. Robert Causey, "Uniform Microreductions," *Synthese*, xxv (1972): 176–218, p. 176; references to Causey will be to this article unless otherwise noted. See also his "Attribute-Identities in Microreductions," *Journal of Philosophy*, LXIX (1972): 407–422; "Identities and Reduction: A Reply," *Noûs*, x (1976): 333–337.

for reductions; no theory relates water molecules and H_2O structures, except insofar as we claim that they are one and the same (203–211).

Causey makes one additional refinement of the traditional derivational view. Nagel leaves the precise character of the set of connecting assumptions something of a mystery; Causey proposes that we speak of a minimal set of bridge laws: a set of connecting assumptions is *minimal* if and only if it "is adequate to accomplish the reduction but any proper subset of [it] is inadequate to accomplish the reduction"(212). Causey's point responds to a bit of vagueness on Nagel's part, though, once we view connecting assumptions as biconditionals in form, it may seem trivial. Russell's requirement of eliminability requires that there be a biconditional for each term of the reduced theory; unambiguous eliminability requires that there be only one such biconditional.

2. *The Counterfactual Model*

All these objections to and modifications of the basic derivational paradigm have accepted the central framework of the account while trying to refine more peripheral features. A more radical criticism of the derivational account holds that the relationship between two theories involved in reduction is not one of logical entailment, and that in fact the theory to be reduced is generally logically incompatible with the reducing theory. Sometimes it is said simply that the reduced theory approximates the reducing theory, but, in any case, the theories contradict each other. The fact that many of the reductions in the history of science fit this view quite readily has been used to discredit not only the derivational account of reduction but the deductive model of explanation as well.[9]

Unquestionably many reductions in empirical science have involved theories inconsistent with one another; but what significance does this have for reductions involving theories with ostensible commitments to abstract entities, for example, mathematical theories, or even physical theories that

9. This model, in some form or other, has been advanced by Schaffner, p. 144; Sklar, p. 11; Glymour, p. 340; Hempel, p. 190; Paul K. Feyerabend, "Explanation, Reduction, and Empiricism," *Minnesota Studies in the Philosophy of Science* III (Minneapolis: University of Minnesota Press, 1962): 28–97; Thomas S. Kuhn, *The Structure of Scientific Revolutions* (Chicago: University of Chicago Press, 1962); Karl R. Popper, "The Aim of Science," *Ratio,* I (1957): 24–35; Popper, "Truth, Rationality, and the Growth of Scientific Knowledge," in *Conjecture and Refutations* (New York: Basic Books, 1962): 215–250; and even Kemeny and Oppenheim, p. 13.

contain them? In a historical sense, it may have great relevance; Imre Lakatos has stressed the similarity between the development of mathematics and the development of empirical sciences in terms of theory construction, testing, and revision.[10] Some reductions in mathematics, for example, Lakatos' case of the treatment of the problem of polyhedra in vector algebra, fit this paradigm. Nevertheless, this problem differs from that encountered by the philosopher who asks whether arithmetic reduces to set theory on some particular formulation. Nagel stipulates that we should demand explicitness in reduction, in the sense that the theories involved must be suitably formalized.[11] In mathematics we can achieve this to an extent far greater than in most contexts in empirical science. In asking about the ontological commitments of a theory we ask about a given theory at a given moment, not about the development of some theory over time. So when we inquire about the reducibility of a mathematical theory and are interested in the ontological implications of the answer, we are concerned with a theory that is "frozen" at that time and with its relation to some other "frozen" theory. This static conception of reduction does not permit that the theories involved be incompatible. Consider, for example, the "reduction" of Newtonian mechanics to relativistic mechanics. These theories logically contradict each other; mass is independent of motion on Newton's theory, but varies with motion according to Einstein's. Though it is interesting historically that we can obtain Newton's theory by letting certain factors in relativistic equations go to zero or to infinity, this does not convince us that there is any ontological moral to be drawn from the reductive relationship. In fact, we tend to think that Newton's theory is false—though we continue to use and study it for other reasons—and that relativistic mechanics has *replaced* the Newtonian theory.

We can clarify this by treating the model on its own terms. Sklar draws a distinction between explaining a theory and explaining a theory's success. When a reduction takes place, the new theory—if it does not directly explain the old by being related to it logically by way of the Nagel paradigm— explains the *success* of the old theory by explaining why the theory worked as well as it did, how closely the old theory approximated the new theory, etc.; we may claim, then, that two theories contradict each other, that one reduces the

10. See *Proofs and Refutations* (New York: Cambridge, 1976).

11. *The Structure of Science*, p. 345; see Schaffner, p. 139.

other, and yet that the one does not explain the other (112–123). Some theories we retain as correct, or very nearly so, after a reduction; others we discard. These theories may be said to be replaced rather than reduced. The retention of theories after reduction we may consider, according to Sklar, an indication of their success as calculating devices. We continue to study Newtonian mechanics, for example, because it provides us with a very good approximation to the truth within certain very frequently employed parameters.

Thomas Nickles draws a distinction between domain-combining and domain-preserving reductions: a domain-combining reduction "is the achievement of postulational and ontological economy and is obtained chiefly by derivational reduction as described by Nagel; i.e., reduction$_1$ amounts to the *explanation* of one theory by another."[12] A domain-preserving reduction (or reduction$_2$) does not achieve any postulational or ontological economy, and fits the model advocated by Feyerabend, Kuhn, *et al.*, better than it does the Nagel model of reduction as derivation. Reduction$_2$ involves two theories that are logically incompatible with each other, and one reduces to the other by way of special assumptions, limiting cases, etc. (Compare the reduction of Newtonian to relativistic mechanics.) Nickles holds these to be two quite different models of reduction, not merely an exact and an approximate version of the same basic concept. There may be exact *and* approximate reductions that fall into either the domain-combining or the domain-preserving categories.[13] The sort of reduction Nickles considers to have any ontological significance is derivational. Any other sort holds little interest for the project of elucidating ontological reduction in mathematics or in other theories involving abstract objects. Nickles suggests that both the derivational and counterfactual models reflect actual types of reduction in science, which have different philosophical implications and which bear on different scientific contexts; his domain-combining reductions are similar to Russellian reductions in mathematical realms.

Clark Glymour offers yet another account of those cases in science which are characterized by incompatible theories standing in reductive relationships. Glymour holds that even these reductions are derivational, with the peculiar feature

---

12. "Two Concepts of Intertheoretic Reduction," *Journal of Philosophy,* LXX (1973): 181–201, p. 181.

13. Nickles, pp. 195–6; see also pp. 181, 184–186.

that some of the connecting assumptions are not assertions of fact but assertions of fiction, that is, counterfactuals. Intertheoretic explanation is thus not the simple explanation of one theory by another, nor is it the explanation of a theory's success; it is an explanation of the circumstances under which the theory in question would be true, even though it is false in the actual world. Thus "a theory is explained by showing under what conditions it would be true, and by contrasting these conditions with the conditions which actually obtain."[14] We may derive truths of Newtonian mechanics, for example, by supplementing relativistic laws with the assumption—the *counterfactual* assumption—that the speed of light is infinite. The Einsteinian law "$N = M + K/C^2$" thus becomes "$N = M$", an assertion that inertial mass and rest mass are identical; the term relating inertial mass to kinetic energy is eliminated. From a formal point of view, therefore, intertheoretic explanation "consists first, in the connection of the terms of the secondary theory with those in the primary theory by means of syntactic definitions; and second, in the generation from the primary theory, by means of deduction, special assumptions, limiting procedures and possibly other devices, of a collection of sentences which, together with the definitions, entails the secondary theory."[15] How does this account differ from the derivational account of Russell or Nagel? Leaving aside all but the formal aspects of reduction, the answer is that the counterfactual assumptions are the only features of Glymour's analysis distinguishing it from a straightforwardly derivational account.

This helps us in contemplating the nature of reduction in mathematics or in other abstract theories, for in these contexts the notion of a counterfactual does not make much sense. One might think of geometry as an instance of entertaining possibly counterfactual assumptions concerning the curvature of space, but, insofar as we do this, we are doing applied geometry or physics rather than pure mathematics. In general, mathematics is characterized by its universality and its necessity. Mathematical statements, it is often thought, must be true in all possible worlds if they are true at all. But if we adopt this conception of mathematics, then the notion of a counterfactual assumption in mathemat-

14. Glymour, p. 341. For a similar view see Wilfrid Sellars, "The Language of Theories," in *Science, Perception, and Reality* (London: Routledge & Kegan Paul, 1963): 106–126.

15. Glymour, p. 343; see also pp. 341–343, 352.

ics is incoherent. What we retain, if we abstract from the counterfactual model of reduction its counterfactual elements, is the familiar derivational account of reduction.

3. The Model-theoretic Model

Patrick Suppes has advanced another, rather different model of reduction in science, which I shall call the *model-theoretic* model. Suppes offers the following account: T reduces to T' if, for every model of T, it is possible to construct an isomorphic model of T'.[16] Now it is difficult to evaluate this paradigm because of its vagueness: Suppes refuses to articulate any general account of what an "isomorphism" is. We may make the model a bit more precise, however, by filling in the standard definition of "isomorphism" as it is used in model theory. Think of a model as a structured set, i.e., as an ordered pair (K,N), K being a set of objects and N a set of relations each of which has a field $K_0 \subseteq K$. Then two models (K,N) and (K',N') are *isomorphic* if and only if there are one-to-one mappings f and g of K onto K' and N onto N', respectively, such that, for every n-tuple of members of K, $<x_1, \ldots, x_n>$, and for every n-ary relation R of N, $R <_1, \ldots, x_n>$ if and only if $R' <x_1', \ldots, x_n'>$, where x_i' and R' are the images of x_i and R under f and g, respectively.

The Suppes conception of reduction has a number of rather odd features. First, normally we do not think that there is anything wrong with speaking of number theory as reducible to set theory, even though the domain of set theory is much larger than the domain of arithmetic. But isomorphism entails equicardinality, so such a reduction appears to be impossible. To correct the difficulty one might speak of the reducibility of arithmetic to a part of set theory, though this would force rejection of the principle that, if T is reducible to T', then T can be reduced to any supertheory of T'. Schaffner instead alters the definition of reduction so that it requires that, for any model of T, there is a model of T' such that from it we can construct another model isomorphic to the model of the reduced theory T (141, 145). In other words, if the model of set theory is too large, we restrict its domain to one which is equicardinal with the domain of the model of arithmetic in question, correspondingly restricting the relations as well.

Second, Schaffner has shown that, if a Nagel reduction is possible between two theories, a Suppes reduction is also possible (145). Thus the Suppes paradigm is weaker than the

---

16. Suppes, *Introduction to Logic* (Princeton: Van Nostrand, 1957), p. 271.

derivational model; the converse does not hold. Imagine a theory with two simple postulates:

$$(x)(Fxx)$$
$$(\exists x)(y)(x = y)$$

and a second theory, also with two postulates:

$$(\exists x)(\exists y)((x \neq y) \,\&\, (z)(z = x \lor z = y))$$
$$(x)(y)(Gxy)$$

We may represent a model of the first theory very easily: let the single object in the domain of the theory be a. Then $K = \{a\}$, and $N = \{<a,a>\}$. We can characterize a model for the second theory as follows: $K' = \{b,c\}$; $N' = \{<b,b>, <b,c>, <c,b>, <c,c>\}$. Now restrict this model to the domain with the single object b. The result is a model obviously isomorphic to that presented for the first theory. Thus, on the Suppes paradigm, the first theory reduces to the second. But it is clear that we can construct no derivational reduction; the two theories are logically incompatible. The Suppes model thus seems to be too weak to reflect the nature of reduction, on formal grounds alone.

4. *The Explanatory Model*

The last model of reduction as a scientific activity I shall discuss is the model Kemeny and Oppenheim present in their famous 1956 paper. I call this account the *explanatory* model because it rejects translatability and eliminability as central to reduction and insists instead on the significance of explanatory power. Kemeny and Oppenheim define reduction as "a certain type of progress in science" (6), and as a result their portrait assimilates reduction to a kind of theoretical advance. Of course, this sort of advance can take place only if the new theory explains all that the old theory did; hence the notion of explanatory power becomes significant. Furthermore, implicit in this view is a distinction between what is to be explained, by one theory or another, and what does the explaining. The view espoused by Kemeny and Oppenheim is thus committed at its very roots to some form of the observational-theoretical dichotomy.[17] The account, in short, is this. T is reducible to T', if T contains some term not in T', T' is capable of explaining all the data explained by T,

---

17. Cf. Kemeny and Oppenheim, pp. 13-4; Sklar, pp. 114-5.

and T' is at least as well systematized as T. The problems with this become evident when we try to extend it to mathematical contexts. First, it is hard to know what an observational-theoretical distinction would be like in mathematics; one is reminded of views holding that basic arithmetical statements such as '1 + 1 = 2', or even '1 = 1', function as observation statements which must be explained by a theory, namely, arithmetic. This view is so peculiar that it is hard to refute. Any theory that does not explain all the "data" that arithmetic normally explains will not do as a reducing theory, but on grounds quite open to the derivational theorist: not all the theorems will be preserved under the reductive transformation. Russell did tend to think of arithmetical statements as data to be reconstructed in his reduction of arithmetic to set theory; if this is all we mean by such a view, however, the explanation is done by the relations between the "data" and the theory introduced to explain them. On Kemeny and Oppenheim's view, these relations would be deductive. Thus, the model on this interpretation melts into the derivational account. Second, the systematization requirement is fairly trivial in mathematics, which is generally much more formalized than empirical science. We might, of course, take axiomatizability, decidability, completeness, etc., as signs of "systematic power". But in that case reductions would be possible only if the theories inhabited the same category with respect to systematic power; for the condition would prevent, for example, a decidable theory from being reduced to an undecidable theory. I shall argue later, however, that no undecidable theory should be reducible to a decidable theory. It is clear, nonetheless, that reduction should be able to cross such boundaries. Any subtheory, for instance, should reduce to a supertheory by way of the identity mapping. But undecidable theories often have decidable subtheories (e.g., first-order logic and the propositional calculus). One might argue that *un*axiomatizability, *un*decidability, and *in*completeness contribute to systematic power; in some contexts, the provability of a completeness theorem may seem to be a limiting result. To an extent, the derivational paradigm respects this position. We shall see in the next chapter that reductive relations imply, roughly, a "transfer" of such properties as completeness, decidability, and even consistency, though no such result is forthcoming for axiomatizability and related concepts. But the addition of such a condition does not help to demarcate the boundaries of successful reduction very clearly; furthermore, this interpretation surely diverges widely from the intentions of Kemeny and Oppenheim in framing their notion of systematic power. The "explanatory" model, therefore, offers little toward the understanding of ontological reduction involving theories with ostensible commitments to abstract entities.

We have seen that the derivational account of reduction in science corresponds closely to the analysis of reduction developed by Russell and Carnap, once we remove the characteristically empirical elements and examine the implications of the account for reductions involving abstract entities. The counterfactual account either describes a kind of reduction that has no ontological significance, or is itself derivational, with the oddity that some of the connecting assumptions between the theories may be counterfactuals. Since the notion of a counterfactual with respect to abstract objects makes little sense, the counterfactual model on this interpretation folds into the derivational model. The model-theoretic model, as we have seen, is too weak to mirror what we mean by ontological reduction, and the Kemeny-Oppenheim model rests on distinctions and assumptions limited to the field of empirical theories, with no abstract counterparts. Thus accounts of reduction as a scientific activity either fail to account for reductions involving abstract objects or reinforce the derivational analysis of reduction with regard to them.

4 Reduction and Interpretability

In this chapter I shall look to formal treatments of the logic of intertheoretic relationships for guidance in developing an adequate account of ontological reduction for theories involving ostensible commitments to abstract objects. I shall examine a variety of concepts which have arisen from technical problems involving consistency and undecidability, and single out one of them as an appropriate formalization of the notion we have been trying to capture. Finally I shall investigate the logic of this notion, proving some elementary theorems concerning reductive relations.

1. Consistency and Undecidability Proofs

Throughout the history of mathematics, significant advances have been made by introducing concepts that have been treated initially with suspicion. Irrational numbers, imaginary numbers, and infinite cardinals come to mind as examples of objects that have aroused controversy when first proposed. The resolution of these controversies has required, in effect, providing foundations for the new branches of mathematics which arose from the introduction of these objects. Hilbert formulated this problem as one of consistency, maintaining that the new branch of mathematics should be formalized so that the notion of 'provable in the system' is made precise, and then that a proof should be constructed which would demonstrate that not all formulas can be proved in the system. Of course, absolute consistency proofs of this sort are extremely hard to come by, and even then can be achieved only at great expense, as Gödel has shown. So the technique of providing a *relative* consistency proof for some suspect portion of mathematics has attained substantial importance. Suppose that '*I*' represents the theory of imaginary numbers, and '*T*' a theory we feel comfortable with, or relatively so. Instead of showing directly that I is consistent, we show that, if T is consistent, then so is I. The translation of non-Euclidean geometry to Euclidean geometry devised by Poincaré, the famous proof of Klein, and the proofs by Gödel and Cohen of the consistency and independence, respectively, of the continuum hypothesis stand out as brilliant applications of this general strategy. Furthermore, each of these proofs relies on translation: specifically, translation of the theory in question into some more readily acceptable theory. Ever since Gödel's famous proof of the undecidability of arithmetic was published in 1931, questions concerning decidability and undecidability have also taken on tremendous significance for mathematical logic.[1] A theory is *decidable* if and only if the set of its theorems is recursive. Because of the increased importance of this notion, it has become worthwhile to develop techniques for proving the decidability or undecidability (i.e., for solving the *decision problem*) of various theories. Once again, translation has provided the cornerstone for such techniques. As in the case of consistency problems, absolute undecidability proofs are very hard to achieve; we thus settle for a relative undecidability proof, which shows that, if some well-known theory T is undecidable, then the theory in question is also undecidable.[2] Ideally, of course, we will possess an absolute solution to the decision problem for our well-known theory; so the relative proof will yield an absolute conclusion concerning the decidability of the theory at hand.

Why should decision problems hold any interest for the philosopher investigating ontological reduction? A simple argument, which I shall formalize later, may convince us that there is a connection between problems of decidability and reducibility. Suppose that an undecidable theory T were reducible to a decidable theory T'. Then the decision procedure that allows us to recognize the theorems of T' would apparently allow us to recognize theorems of T, granted that the translation between the theories were itself recursive and theorem-preserving. Since T-theorems would become T'-

1. See Kurt Gödel, "On Formally Undecidable Propositions of *Principia Mathematica* and Related Systems I," in Jean van Heijenoort, ed., *From Frege to Gödel* (Cambridge, Mass.: Harvard, 1967), pp. 596–616.

2. Decidability proofs do not give rise to the same problems as proofs of undecidability. Though we could, perhaps, use a relative proof to demonstrate decidability, most often we simply exhibit a decision procedure. Thus decidability does not, in general, depend upon consistency, the decidability of some other theory, or Church's thesis. Undecidability proofs, on the other hand, mean to show that the set of theorems of some theory is not recursive; they must therefore presuppose consistency (for otherwise the set of theorems would be the set of formulas, a recursive class) and Church's thesis (to link nonrecursiveness to the absence of an effective decision procedure), in addition to assumptions about the undecidability of other theories. I owe thanks to Charles Parsons for bringing the asymmetry between decidability and undecidability proofs to my attention.

theorems under such a translation, the recursive character of the set of T'-theorems would guarantee that the set of T-theorems was recursive. In fact, there are some subtleties that this argument overlooks; in general, nevertheless, and with some qualifications, no undecidable theory should reduce to a decidable one. Reductive translations thus aid in solving the decision problem in two ways. For any theory T, if T can be translated into a decidable theory, then (with some qualifications) T is decidable; if an undecidable theory can be translated into T, then again with qualifications, T is undecidable.

There is an analogous connection between consistency and reducibility. Suppose that an inconsistent theory S were reducible to a consistent theory S'. The terms of S would be dispensable in favor of the terms of S', in such a way that the theorems of S would become theorems of S'. But since S is inconsistent, *any* S-formula is a theorem of S, so all the translations of these formulas would have to be theorems of S'. In particular, there would be a pair of formulas, A and $-A$, both of which were theorems of S; their translations would have to be theorems of S'. But so long as the translation were to preserve negation, S' would be inconsistent. Thus, if our conception of reduction preserves negation, that S reduces to S' entails that, if S' is consistent, S must be consistent as well.

I shall examine a series of concepts, roughly in order of increasing strength, which mathematical logicians have developed for use in relative proofs of consistency and undecidability. I shall reject both the weakest and the strongest notions, and argue that, as might have pleased Aristotle, the correct formalization of ontological reduction lies somewhere in the middle. Throughout this examination, I shall deal with syntactic concepts of reduction, for the sake of simplicity and ease of expression. I shall also work most frequently with arithmetized theories, so that logical functions will be arithmetical functions, with Gödel numbers standing in for formulas. The arithmetized conceptions of reduction are most useful from a technical point of view, though the Gödel numbering makes no difference given our interest in the ontological significance of the notions.

First, let us consider a notion Georg Kreisel develops for use in relative consistency proofs. A recursive function $t(n)$, Kreisel says, is an *(S)-translation* of S_1 into S_2 if

$$\vdash_S (\exists y) \text{ Prov}_1 (y, n) \supset (\exists y) \text{ Prov}_2 (y, t(n))$$

and

$$\vdash_S t(v_1(n)) = v_2(t(n)) \text{ (if } n \text{ is a formula of } S_1).[3]$$

Here $v_i(n)$ is the Gödel number for the negation of the formula n in S_i. We may read the definition, then, as saying that $t(n)$ is an (S)-translation of S_1 into S_2 just in case (1) if there is a y that is the Gödel number of a proof in S_1 of n, then there is a y that is the Gödel number of a proof of $t(n)$ in S_2, and (2) the image of the negation of n is identical with the negation of the image of n. To dearithmetize this definition, imagine the translation t as a function from formulas of S_1, the language of the theory T_1, into S_2, the language of the theory T_2. Then t is an (S)-translation just in case (1) for any S_1-formula A, if A is an element of T_1, then $t(A)$ is an element of T_2; and (2) for any S_1-formula A, $t(-A) = -t(A)$. The translation thus takes formulas into formulas, preserving under the translation nothing but theoremhood and negations.

Kreisel's concept of an (S)-translation is very weak, but it nevertheless has the relationship we want it to have with consistency. In fact, it is probably the weakest translation-type relation having this character; for negation and theorem preservation are the minimal requirements for generating a relative consistency proof. Translatability implies relative consistency, though the converse relationship does not hold. Suppose that T can be translated into T'. T' must entail T when the requisite transformations on the formulas of T have been carried out. (Note that these transformations are theorem-preserving.) Now suppose that T were inconsistent. T' can entail a theorem-preserving transformation of T only if T' itself is inconsistent. Thus the translatability of T into T' shows that, if T is inconsistent, T' is inconsistent; the translation implies, in other words, that if T' is consistent, T must be also.

Still, we have reason to deny that (S)-translation provides an adequate formal representation of reduction. In general, the translation of a formula under this schema weakens the formula; the translation does not, according to Kreisel, "express the full content" of the original formula (32). As a re-

3. "Models, Translations and Interpretations," in Thoralf Skolem, ed., *Mathematical Interpretations of Formal Systems* (Amsterdam: North-Holland, 1955), pp. 30–1.

sult, the translation from S_1 into S_2 provides little or no information about these systems other than that concerning their relative consistency relations. Consider, for instance, the "reduction" of the predicate calculus to the propositional calculus by way of a translation showing, in effect, that every theorem of the predicate calculus is true in a universe consisting of a single individual. Since these formulas can then be expressed in the propositional calculus, the consistency of the propositional calculus implies the consistency of the predicate calculus. But surely this is not a reduction in the sense in which we are interested. We have demonstrated no ontological connection between the predicate and propositional calculi; indeed, since there almost certainly is no such link, the use of translation in Kreisel's sense as a model for ontological reduction would amount to nothing more than a sham.

Second, I shall examine a concept which Tarski has called *weak interpretability*. This notion, too, we shall find to be too weak to characterize adequately the concept of ontological reduction. In order to evaluate it, however, we must explore a slightly wider area. Tarski employs three notions to clarify the relationship between the decision problem and questions of reduction or translation: interpretability, weak interpretability, and relative interpretability. All three have important links with undecidability-proof techniques. Which of these notions, if any, elucidates the nature of reduction?

To define any of these terms, we must introduce the concept of a possible definition. Let us assume that the only nonlogical symbols in the theories concerned are predicate symbols; we can eliminate individual constants, function symbols, etc., in favor of these in familiar ways. A possible definition of an n-ary predicate constant F in a theory T to which F does not belong is a universalized biconditional of the form:

$$(x_1) \ldots (x_n) \, (F(x_1, \ldots, x_n) \equiv \varphi)$$

where φ is a formula of T.[4] Now let T and T' be any two theories, and, to simplify matters, assume that they have no nonlogical constants in common. T is *interpretable* in T' if it is possible to extend T' by including in the set of theorems some possible definitions of the nonlogical constants of T, in

4. Alfred Tarski, "A General Method in Proofs of Undecidability," in Tarski, A. Mostowski, and R. Robinson, *Undecidable Theories* (Amsterdam: North-Holland, 1953), p. 20. Further parenthetical page references to Tarski will be to this work, unless otherwise noted.

such a way that the resulting theory is an extension not only of T' but of T as well. To make this more precise, T_2 is interpretable in T_1 if and only if there is a theory T and a set D satisfying the following conditions: (1) T is a common extension of T_1 and T_2, and every constant (i.e., predicate) of T is a constant of T_1 or T_2; (2) D is a recursive set of sentences which are theorems of T and which are possible definitions in T_1 of nonlogical constants of T_2; (3) each nonlogical constant of T_2 occurs in just one sentence of D; and (4) every theorem of T is derivable in T from a set of sentences each of which is a theorem of T_1 or belongs to D (21). We can see that, if T_2 is interpretable in T_1, then any subtheory of T_2 is interpretable in any extension of T_1. Also, interpretability is transitive: if T_2 is interpretable in T_1 and T_1 is interpretable in T_0, then T_2 can be interpreted in T_0 as well (22).

A theory T_2 is *weakly interpretable* in T_1 just in case T_2 is interpretable in some consistent extension of T_1 having the same predicates as T_1. Thus T_2 is weakly interpretable in T_1 if and only if T_1 and T_2 have a consistent common extension T satisfying the following condition: there is a recursive set D of theorems of T such that, for every nonlogical constant C of T_2 which does not occur in T_1, some possible definition of C in T_1 belongs to D (21–2). This paradigm requires definability, one might say, but not derivability. Any predicate of the reduced theory must have a definition in the terms of the reducing theory, but there is no demand that all the theorems of the reduced theory go into theorems of the reducing theory; some may go into theorems of T that are not elements of $T_1 \cup T_2 \cup D$, for we have made no restriction on the theory T except that it be some extension of T_1 and T_2, with the satisfaction of a definability condition.

With Tarski, we may note further that weak interpretability is not a transitive relation (22). This alone creates grave doubt about its ability to represent formally a notion of ontological reduction. Recall that the "in principle" clauses found in the reductive programs of Russell and Carnap require that relations of reduction be transitive; in general we cannot, from a practical point of view, eliminate at once all discourse but that of the basis of a constructional system. Instead, a constructional system introduces a quasi-ordering of the objects or predicates of a system into levels according to their proximity to the system's basis. One demonstrates, for example, that the objects of level 9 are reducible to those of level 8, that those of level 8 can be reduced to those of level 7, etc., concluding that all these objects can in fact be reduced to those of level 0, the basis of the system. But this conclusion does not follow unless the reducibility relation is transitive. Tarski's weak interpretability, then, proves to be *too* weak to stand as a formal representative of the notion of reduction.

Third, let us examine Tarski's concept of interpretability. We have already presented Tarski's definition, but for the sake of clarity and future comparison, it may be helpful to alter the form of the definition, without of course changing the concept. We may say that an interpretation I is an interpretation from s_2 into s_1 if and only if I is a recursive function from s_2-predicates into s_1-formulas and s_2-formulas into s_1-formulas such that

$$I(R(x_1, \ldots, x_n)) = I\ (R)\ (x_1, \ldots, x_n)$$
$$I(-A) = -I(A)$$
$$I(A\ \&\ B) = I(A)\ \&\ I(B)$$
$$I((x)A) = (x)I(A)$$

This corresponds to Kreisel's concept of modeling. He observes that

> The familiar consistency proofs of various geometries, the algebra of complex numbers, or—to take a modern case—of general set theory (G), are obtained by means of models. This notion, which Tarski calls 'interpretation', may be defined for systems of the *first-order predicate calculus* as follows: A system (S_1) has a model in (S_2) if the nonlogical constants of (S_1), i.e. its predicate symbols and function symbols, can be replaced by expressions of (S_2) in such a way that the axioms of (S_1) go into theorems of (S_2).[5]

Kreisel's "having a model in" is thus the same as Tarski's "being interpretable in" but with the possible definitions of Tarski serving as translation rules rather than *bona fide* formulas. In other words, Kreisel takes Tarski's definitions and transfers them to the metalanguage, as I have done in the definition of an interpretation above. We can extend that definition to speak of relations between theories, rather than languages: let us say that an interpretation I from s_2 into s_1 is an *interpretation of* T_2 (in language s_2) *into* T_1 (in language s_1) if and only if, for any s_2-formula A, if A is an element of T_2,

5. Kreisel, p. 28. See also "On the Concepts of Completeness and Interpretation of Formal Systems," *Fundamenta Mathematicae*, xxxix (1952): 103–127.

then $I(A)$ is an element of T_1. Thus T_2 is interpretable in T_1 just in case there is an interpretation of T_2 into T_1.

Whatever Tarski's intentions, Kreisel clearly intends this to capture the traditional derivational model of reduction: "Frege, Russell and others developed the theory of classes to provide foundations for (pretty diverse) logical systems; and by this they meant that a model could be constructed for the system by terms of the theory of classes."[6] Does interpretability succeed in mirroring an adequate concept of ontological reduction?

Consider for a moment the Zermelo mapping of the numbers into set theory. Zero is mapped into the null set, {}, 1 into {{}}, 2 into {{{}}}, etc. Now suppose we have some set-theoretic expression that defines the number-theoretic predicate 'even': whatever this looks like, it will be true of just those representatives of the numbers which, intuitively, have an odd number of left braces ({}, {{{}}}, {{{{}}}}, etc.). Let us symbolize this predicate by '$F(x)$'. Now suppose we likewise have a set-theoretic expression corresponding to the number-theoretic predicate 'odd'; symbolize this by '$G(x)$'. In number theory we want it to be true that every number is either odd or even; so, using the interpretability rubric, we translate this into

$$(x)\ (F(x) \vee G(x))$$

We have no guarantee, however, that this will be true in set theory. Presumably we have taken pains to sort the sets that represent the numbers into even and odd categories, but we have no guarantee that we have thereby categorized *every* set as odd or even. Moreover, it is hard to see why we should need to provide such a guarantee; finding a set-theoretic predicate that does what we want with the representatives of the numbers seems to be enough. It would seem more natural, then, to use the translation

$$(x)\ (N(x) \supset (F(x) \vee G(x)))$$

where '$N(x)$' is used to pick out the relevant domain, in this instance, the set of sets that represent the numbers under the mapping. When we are concerned with reducing a theory to another whose domain is of the same cardinality, the difference between these translation rubrics may be insignificant.

6. "On the Concepts of Completeness and Interpretation of Formal Systems," p. 104.

But in cases in which we want to reduce a theory to one with a larger domain, the relativizing predicate helps to single out the portion of the larger domain taken as representing the smaller one. And since that subset of the domain is all we have interest in, as a representation of the reduced domain, we have no philosophical reason not to restrict our attention to that subset in the quantificational formulas.

Fourth, I shall examine Tarski's concept of *relative interpretability*[7]. We may say that T_2 is *relatively interpretable* in T_1 if and only if the correlated theory $T_2^{(P)}$, obtained by relativizing T_2 to a predicate P which does not occur in T_2, is interpretable in T_1 in the usual sense (29). The set of predicates of the relativized theory $T_2^{(P)}$ consists of all the predicates of T_2, in addition to the single predicate P; the relativization of an arbitrary formula A of T_2 proceeds by replacing every subformula of the form $(x)B$ or $(\exists x)B$ by the expressions (x) $(Px \supset B)$ or $(\exists x)$ $(Px \mathbin{\&} B)$, respectively (24-5). Tarski's discussion of the relativized theory may confuse the presentation of relative interpretability more than it helps; we may spell out the notion in a more direct way. $I = (f,d)$ is a *relative interpretation* from s_2 into s_1 if and only if d is a unary predicate and f is a recursive function from s_2-predicate constants into s_1-formulas satisfying the following conditions:

$$I(Rx_1, \ldots, x_n) = f(R) (x_1, \ldots, x_n)$$
$$I(-A) = -I(A)$$
$$I(A \mathbin{\&} B) = I(A) \mathbin{\&} I(B)$$
$$I((x)A) = (x) (dx \supset I(A))$$

7. There are concepts between weak and relative interpretability, or between (S)-translation and relative interpretability, which I have omitted from this discussion. The most important are parametrical interpretability, partially ordered interpretability, and d-dimensional interpretability. For parametrical interpretability, see N. Motohashi, "Partially Ordered Interpretations," *Journal of Symbolic Logic*, XLII (1977): 83–93; P. Hájek, "Syntactic Models of Axiomatic Theories," *Bulletin de l'Académie Polonaise des Sciences*, LXXI (1951): 273–278; "Generalized Interpretability in Terms of Models," *Casopis pro pestavani matematiki*, XCI (1966): 352–357; U. Felgner, *Models of ZF-Set Theory* (Berlin: Springer-Verlag, 1971). For partially ordered interpretability, see Motohashi, *op. cit.*; for d-dimensional interpretations, see Jan Mycielski, "A Lattice of Interpretability Types of Theories," *Journal of Symbolic Logic*, XLII (1977): 297–305. I reject these as representatives of ontological reduction on two grounds: (1) they appear to be nonelementary—see L. W. Szczerba, "Interpretability of Elementary Theories," in R. Butts and J. Hintikka, eds., *Logic, Foundations of Mathematics and Computability Theory* (Boston: Reidel, 1977): 129–145—for they seem to slip portions of set theory or second-order logic into the concept of interpretability; (2) methodologically, they appear to admit too much logical machinery, without prior ontological scrutiny. But a full discussion of these issues would take us far afield.

An interpretation I from s_2 into s_1 is a *relative interpretation* of T_2 (in language s_2) *into* T_1 (in language s_1) if and only if, for any s_2-formula A, either A is not an element of T_2 or $I(A)$ is an element of T_1. Thus we say that T_2 is relatively interpretable in T_1 just in case there is some relative interpretation of T_2 into T_1.

Relative interpretability arises naturally, therefore, from the discussion of interpretability as a representative of relations of ontological reducibility. Though Tarski's discussion makes the difference between the two concepts seem considerable, we can now see that relative interpretability differs from interpretability only by relativizing the quantificational clause of the definition to some unary predicate d. Relative interpretability is slightly weaker than interpretability as a result: any interpretation is a relative interpretation, but only certain relative interpretations (namely, those where d performs no work, i.e., is such that $T_1 \vdash (x)\ dx$) are interpretations.

We have finally reached a notion that comes very close to explicating the conception of reduction developed by Russell and Carnap. In Tarski's terms, D is a set of possible definitions, of universalized biconditional form, with exactly one formula for every constant appearing in the reduced, but not the reducing theory. (Tarski makes the assumption that the theories involved have no predicate constants in common, but this is no real restriction: we may assign dummy letters to the constants of the reduced theory which also appear in the reducing theory and then link the dummies to the original predicates by way of possible definitions.) The reduced theory is logically derivable from the reducing theory, and, since the "connecting assumptions" are biconditionals and provide a recursive link between the definiens and the definiendum, the vocabulary of the reduced theory can be eliminated. The translation, furthermore, preserves theoremhood. Both interpretability and its relativized cousin are transitive relations; both deal with uninterpreted rather than interpreted theories, and so risk running afoul of Russell's account on those grounds. But relative interpretability has the advantage of allowing us to reduce a theory to one with a larger domain, by carving out the relevant portion of that universe with the relativizing predicate and talking about that portion alone.

It appears, then, that relative interpretability represents formally the notion of ontological reduction which we have been seeking. I have already argued in chapter two that theorem preservation is a necessary and sufficient condition for one theory's following from another, in the sense in which Russell, for example, means that mathematics follows from logic. Russell and Carnap, however, insist not on theorem preservation but on truth-value preservation, which is more stringent. Relative interpretability guarantees that theorems go into theorems, but not that all nontheorems go into nontheorems. Should we strengthen our account to make such a demand?

Finally, then, I shall discuss *strong interpretability*. Intuitively, strong interpretability is interpretability together with the requirement that nontheorems go into nontheorems. We may similarly define *strong relative interpretability* as relative interpretability with the same additional requirement. To formalize this conception, we may say that T_2 is *strongly interpretable* in T_1 just in case there is an interpretation from the language of T_2 into the language of T_1 such that, if A is a theorem of T_2, then $I(A)$ is a theorem of T_1, and, if A is not a theorem of T_2, then $I(A)$ is not a theorem of T_1, for any formula A in the language of T_2. That is, A is a theorem of T_2 *if and only if $I(A)$ is a theorem of T_1*. We should note, incidentally, that though this introduces an element of symmetry into the definition of interpretation, it is not equivalent to mutual interpretability: we cannot show that T_2 is strongly interpretable in T_1 just in case T_2 and T_1 are interpretable in one another.[8] The situation with strong relative interpretability is of course analogous.

I shall argue that the symmetry makes strong interpretability (and its relative counterpart) inappropriate for representing the derivational model of ontological reduction. First, should a theory ever be reducible to one that will give rise to new theorems, even in the original language of the reduced theory? Consider the case of an empirical theory, say thermodynamics, which reduces to another empirical theory, say statistical mechanics. We can translate thermodynamics into statistical mechanics in such a way that the theorems of thermodynamics become laws of statistical mechanics.[9]

8. A counterexample is the relationship between Peano arithmetic and the theory consisting of Peano arithmetic supplemented by the negation of the arithmetized consistency statement for PA. PA ∪ {−Con PA} is interpretable in PA, and similarly PA can be interpreted in PA ∪ {−Con PA} (in fact, trivially so). But PA is not strongly interpretable in PA ∪ {−Con PA}. See Solomon Feferman, "Arithmetization of Metamathematics in a General Setting," *Fundamenta Mathematicae*, XLIX (1960): 35–92, pp. 39, 77.

9. In fact, reductive relations involving empirical theories are rarely quite so neat. See above, chapter three; also Kenneth Schaffner, "Approaches to Reduction," *Philosophy of Science*, XXXIV (1967): 137–147, pp. 144–5.

Sentences about temperatures we thus translate into sentences about the mean kinetic energy of molecules. Might we not want to allow, however, that some theorems concerning mean kinetic energies might be translatable back into sentences about temperatures that were not theorems of the original theory? In short, the reduction of thermodynamics to statistical mechanics might not only reinterpret sentences about temperatures but also tell us more about temperature itself than we knew beforehand. If we allow the possibility of a reducing theory adding to our knowledge even about the reduced objects taken in themselves, then strong interpretability is not a good formalization of reduction. I urge that we should allow for such a possibility; certainly nothing about that circumstance leads us to say, in the case just considered, that if statistical mechanics tells us more about temperature than we knew before the reduction, then thermodynamics must not be reducible to statistical mechanics after all.

Second, a variety of formal results suggests that strong interpretability, or strong relative interpretability, introduces an inappropriate symmetry into the logic of reductive relationships. Russell and Carnap thought, for example, that any subtheory in a given language should reduce to any supertheory in that language; any subtheory, after all, follows from a supertheory, of which it is a part. Yet it does not turn out that a theory, in general, reduces to any arbitrary supertheory on the strong-interpretability rubric. Results concerning consistency also depart from the model we have been upholding. If T_2 is strongly (relatively) interpretable in T_1, then T_2 is consistent if and only if T_1 is consistent. Other formal relationships are altered as well. As a result, strong interpretability does not prove a useful concept in relative consistency and undecidability proofs; the informal arguments we advanced at the beginning of this chapter, therefore, fail to support the paradigm of strong interpretability. In spite of its initially plausible rendering of Russell's intentions, I urge that we reject strong interpretability as a model of reductive relationships.

2. *Formal Results on Reducibility*

We have thus examined a series of candidates for representing relations of ontological reducibility, rejecting the weakest and the strongest notions and settling upon Tarski's relative interpretability as the most appropriate formalization of that notion. I shall now sharpen that concept somewhat, and prove some simple theorems concerning reducibility relationships.

With some regrets, I shall not retain Tarski's terminology. First, I shall refer to relative interpretability as simply *interpretability*, in keeping with the general practice of contemporary mathematicians.[10] Second, I shall employ Kreisel's technique of transferring the possible definitions of Tarski's scheme into the metalanguage, and so speak of translation functions rather than definitions. Though this is a departure in presentation, it makes no difference from a theoretical point of view. Finally, I shall admit individual constants into the framework; though their omission has been inessential until now, we shall soon consider problems involving the logic of identity. The analysis of these problems will require us to have individual constants in the language.

I shall also depart from Tarski in one way that is not merely terminological. He talks of a relativization to a unary predicate P; I shall instead speak of relativization to a formula with one free variable in the language of the reducing theory. This makes the criterion slightly more stringent in that it requires that the restriction of the domain allowed by the relativization be expressible in the reducing theory. Thus, to consider our case of the reduction of number theory to set theory, we must be able to say in set theory which sets are representing the numbers if we are to be able to take advantage of the domain restriction. This is a minor point, however, for in all the commonly recognized cases of reduction involving relativization the restriction can be so expressed.

We will say that a *theory* is a set of sentences closed under logical consequence. A similarity type will serve as our formal representation of the language of a theory; we will say that a *similarity type s* is a set of individual constants and predicate constants of given -ariness. A theory T is *of* similarity type s if and only if the nonlogical symbols of T, other than individual variables, are exactly those which are elements of s. That T is of the type s we will denote by writing '$T(s)$'.

$I = (f,d)$ is an *interpretation from s_1 into s_2* if and only if d is an s_2-formula with one free variable and f is a recursive function from s_1-predicate constants of n places into s_2-formulas containing n free variables, s_1-individual constants into s_2-individual constants, and individual variables into individual variables such that, where 't', 't_1', 't_n', etc., represent

10. See, for example, Feferman, pp. 49, 71–2; Motohashi, p. 86; Szczerba, p. 133.

terms, that is, either individual constants or individual variables:

$$
\begin{array}{ll}
(1) & I(t) = f(t) = \text{if } t \text{ is a constant} \\
& I(t) = f(t) = t = \text{if } t \text{ is a variable} \\
(2) & I(t_1 = t_2) = (I(t_1) = I(t_2)) \\
(3) & I(R(t_1, \ldots, t_n)) = f(R)\,(I(t_1), \ldots, I(t_n)) \\
(4) & I(-A) = -I(A) \\
(5) & I(A \;\&\; B) = I(A) \;\&\; I(B) \\
(6) & I((x)A) = (x)\,(dx \supset I(A))
\end{array}
$$

An interpretation I from s_1 into s_2 is an *interpretation of* $T_1(s_1)$ *into* $T_2(s_2)$ if and only if, for any s_1-formula A, A is a theorem of T_1 only if $I(A)$ is a theorem of T_2. $T_1(s_1)$ is *interpretable in* T_2 (s_2) *via an interpretation* I *from* s_1 *into* s_2 just in case I is an interpretation of $T_1(s_1)$ into $T_2(s_2)$. [This we will write $'T_1(s_1) \leq_I T_2(s_2)'$.] Finally, $T_1(s_1)$ is *interpretable in* $T_2(s_2)$ if and only if there is an interpretation I such that $T_1(s_1) \leq_I T_2(s_2)$. [This will be written $'T_1(s_1) \leq T_2(s_2)'$.]

We may note a number of simple theorems concerning this conception of interpretability:

Theorem 4.1. The interpretability relation is transitive.

Theorem 4.2. For any theories T and T', if T is a subtheory of T', T is interpretable in T'.

Theorem 4.3. If T is interpretable in T', then any subtheory of T is interpretable in any extension of T'.

The proofs of these theorems are trivial. To explicate the relationship between interpretability and decision problems, we may prove the following:

Theorem 4.4. If T is interpretable in T', then if T' is consistent and decidable, some consistent extension of T is decidable.

Proof: Assume that $T \leq T'$, and that T' is consistent and decidable. Then there is an effective procedure p for recognizing the theorems of T'. Take an arbitrary s-formula A, and construct $I(A)$. If p determines $I(A)$ to be a nontheorem of T', then A is not a theorem of T, by the definition of interpretability. If p determines $I(A)$ to be a theorem of T', then there are two possibilities: (1) A is a theorem of T; (2) neither A nor $-A$ is provable in T. Since T' is consistent, if $I(A)$ is a theorem of T', $-I(A)$ is not a theorem, and so neither is $I(-A)$. But then $-A$ must not be a theorem of T. Therefore, either T is decidable or some consistent extension of T, in the same similarity type, is decidable.

Theorem 4.5. If T is interpretable in T', then, if T is consistent and essentially undecidable, T' is undecidable.

Proof: A theory is said to be *essentially undecidable* if and only if both the theory itself and every consistent extension of the theory with the same constants (i.e., in the same similarity type) are undecidable. This therefore follows quickly from the previous theorem.

Theorem 4.6. If T is interpretable in T', then, if T' is consistent and decidable, and T is complete, T is decidable.

Proof: Assume that $T \le T'$, T' is consistent and decidable, and T is complete. There is then an effective procedure p for recognizing theorems of T'. For an arbitrary s-formula A, if p determines $I(A)$ to be a nontheorem of T', then A is not a theorem of T. If p determines $I(A)$ to be a theorem of T', then by reasoning analogous to that of theorem 4.4, either A is a theorem of T or neither A nor $-A$ is a theorem of T. But in the latter case T is incomplete, contrary to assumption. Therefore, the effective procedure for s'-formulas is also an effective procedure for recognizing T theorems among s-formulas; so T is decidable.

The relationship between consistency and interpretability is spelled out by the next theorem:

Theorem 4.7. If T is interpretable in T', then, if T' is consistent, so is T.

Proof: Assume that T is interpretable in T', and that T' is consistent. Suppose further that T is not consistent. Then, for some s-formulas A and $-A$, A is an element of T and $-A$ is an element of T. Construct $I(A)$, $I(-A)$. Since $T \le T'$, if A is an element of T, $I(A)$ is an element of T', and if $-A$ is an element of T, $I(-A)$ is an element of T'. But $I(-A) = -I(A)$; so T' contains both $I(A)$ and $-I(A)$, and is inconsistent, contrary to assumption.

The following two theorems are derived from Feferman:[11]

Theorem 4.8. For any theories S and T, if Peano arithmetic is a subtheory of S, then T is interpretable in $S \cup \{\text{Con } T\}$ if T has an arithmetically definable set of axioms.

Theorem 4.9. For any supertheory T of Peano arithmetic, $T \cup \{\text{Con } T\}$ is not interpretable in T.

We have examined a variety of concepts with links to proofs of relative consistency and undecidability, singling out one of them as an appropriate formal representation of the notion of ontological reduction we have been seeking. Stronger notions rule out as illegitimate reductions that ought

---

11. See Feferman, theorems 6.2 and 6.5.

to have ontological significance and seem to fit the fundamental derivational paradigm; weaker notions we have rejected as either permitting reductions having no ontological
import (e.g., the reduction of the predicate to the propositional calculus) or refusing to permit some that *do* seem to
have such import. Finally we have proved some basic
theorems concerning interpretability, demonstrating its relation to problems of relative consistency and undecidability.

The concept of interpretability that we have developed in
this chapter assumes that all theories concerned are formulated in some logical system, and in the same logical system,
namely, first-order logic. I have no philosophical reason to
deny that reductions are possible between theories employing other or different logical systems; an intuitionistic theory,
for example, might in some sense reduce to a classical one.
The metatheory of such relationships, however, is highly un-
settled. I have therefore chosen to restrict my attention to the
simpler case, though an extension of the notion of interpretability developed here may be possible.

Interpretability, in the sense articulated in this chapter,
serves as an adequate formal representation of ontological
reduction. Though many philosophers have seen reducibility
as closely related to interpretability, most have made additional requirements: Russell demands special guarantees that
the intended interpretation of a formal theory is being taken
into account, and Quine demands the specification of a proxy
function linking the objects of the reduced to the objects of
the reducing domain.[12] The next several chapters will attempt to show that these demands are not necessary.

12. See W. V. Quine, "Ontological Reduction and the World of Numbers,"
in *The Ways of Paradox and Other Essays* (Cambridge, Mass.: Harvard,
1976): 212–220.

5 Intertheoretic Identifications

In this chapter I shall consider Paul Benacerraf's contention that the uniqueness of a reduction is a necessary condition for its having any philosophical significance. I shall examine his argument in detail, and suggest that he has overlooked a number of crucial alternatives. Finally, I shall construct a semantics for intertheoretic statements in cases of multiple reduction to demonstrate that the account of ontological reduction developed in the previous chapter suffices to deal with circumstances of the kind Benacerraf envisages.

1. *Multiple Reductions*

Quite frequently, one theory reduces to another, if it does so at all, in more than one way. To put the matter somewhat more precisely, the interpretability relations between theories often allow that there is more than one interpretation of the one into the other. In Tarski's terms, several sets of possible definitions may have the desired properties; in Kreisel's terms, more than one mapping will carry all the theorems of the one theory into theorems of the other. When this occurs, I shall say that the first theory is *multiply reducible* to the second, or, to avoid begging any questions that I have postponed to later chapters, that the first is *multiply interpretable* into the second.

The paradigm case of multiply reducible theories is that of the reduction of Peano arithmetic to set theory; Peano arithmetic can be interpreted in set theory by way of the mappings of von Neumann, Zermelo, and Frege and Russell, and in fact by way of infinitely many more. The situation recurs frequently; plane geometry can be reduced to ordered pairs by way of either Cartesian or polar-coordinate mappings, and the rationals and the reals can be constructed from the integers in a variety of ways. Nevertheless, only when abstract entities become involved does this present any philosophical difficulty. In the physical sciences, though such multiple interpretability relations may occur often, there is generally some way of picking out one as the intended interpretation. As Nagel has pointed out, in empirical science the reductive definitions must have empirical support; furthermore, as in the reduction of thermodynamics to statistical mechanics, we intend a microreduction, and so spatiotemporal coincidence provides an important additional criterion which allows us to discard many otherwise acceptable interpretations. With respect to abstract objects, however, these considerations are irrelevant. We cannot subject Tarski's possible definitions, in a given case, to empirical test when the theories concerned are not empirical, nor can we consider spatial or temporal location in attempting to decide between different sets of these definitions when abstract objects are involved.

This might not seem to be a problem at all, except that Clark Glymour, for example, has held that the uniqueness of a reduction is a necessary condition for its having any ontological significance. If we are interested only in interpretability qua interpretability, then the more interpretations having the desired properties, the merrier for the philosopher. But when we are interested in ontology, the following line of thinking might convince us that interpretability relations should not be multiple. Consider the reducibility of arithmetic to set theory. If numbers are really sets, then each number must be some particular set; surely it makes no sense to say that the number 1 is a set, but that no particular set is identical to it. Paul Benacerraf has argued from just this premise that the multiplicity of interpretations of arithmetic in set theory precludes the possibility of numbers really being sets.[1]

The argument generalizes to one that denies that multiple interpretability relations can ever have ontological significance. We may interpret Benacerraf's position, then, as demanding the addition of another condition to our account of ontological reduction; we should add, if Benacerraf is correct, that there must be a unique mapping, or a unique set of possible definitions, which takes theorems into theorems. This demand poses a challenge to our entire project, for the interpretability relations holding between theories of abstract objects are almost invariably multiple. Even the seemingly clearest cases of successful reduction, then, such as that of arithmetic to set theory, or even more basically, that of ordered pairs to unordered sets, will turn out not to have any ontological signficance at all. And in those rare cases where a reduction is apparently unique, it will be extremely difficult

1. Glymour, "On Some Patterns of Reduction," *Philosophy of Science*, XXXVII (1970): 340–353, p. 343; Benacerraf, "What Numbers Could Not Be," *Philosophical Review*, LXXIV (1965): 47–73. Further references to Benacerraf in this chapter will be to this paper, unless noted otherwise.

to prove that no other mapping or set of possible definitions could do the same work.

One way of responding to this challenge is to link it to the problem of interpreting theories, as Russell did. One might argue that we may single out one interpretation as being ontologically significant and discard the others as philosophically uninteresting. As is well known, any progression models the integers;[2] Russell argued that, in spite of this, we can develop a unique analysis of number-theoretic notions by considering not only arithmetic itself but extramathematical or applied contexts as well, such as 'There are n F's'. Russell believed that his own was the correct analysis of number, simply because it explained the extratheoretical use of number-theoretic terms.[3]

W. V. Quine has answered that a consideration of these contexts is unnecessary; as we have seen above, however,[4] his argument claims not that these counting contexts are irrelevant or insignificant, but that we can deal with them easily by invoking the notion of a one-to-one correspondence.[5] Indeed, since we are concerned with ontological reduction and, therefore, want, in Wittgensteinian fashion, to solve the "problem" of a commitment to undesirable abstract objects by showing that the usage of terms supposedly denoting them, and other language purporting to commit us to these entities, can be avoided, we must consider counting and other extratheoretical contexts. To do anything else would be to admit that in some contexts we cannot eliminate these bits of language. Russell was thus right to insist on the importance of these contexts, but wrong to think

2. See, for example, Bertrand Russell, *Introduction to Mathematical Philosophy* (London: Allen & Unwin, 1919), pp. 8–9; *Principles of Mathematics* (New York: Norton, 1903), p. vi; W. V. Quine, *Word and Object* (Cambridge, Mass.: MIT Press, 1960), p. 262; and Benacerraf, p. 56.

3. *Principles of Mathematics*, p. vi; see Hans Reichenbach, "Bertrand Russell's Logic," in Paul A. Schilpp, ed., *The Philosophy of Bertrand Russell* (Evanston: The Library of Living Philosophers, vol. V, 1946): 21–54, pp. 32–3; also Benacerraf, *Logicism: Some Considerations* (Ph.D. dissertation, Princeton University, 1960), p. 159.

4. In chapter two.

5. See *Word and Object*, p. 263; "Ontological Relativity," in *Ontological Relativity and Other Essays* (New York: Columbia University Press, 1969): 26–68, p. 44; "Ontological Reduction and the World of Numbers," in *The Ways of Paradox and Other Essays* (Cambridge, Mass.: Harvard, 1976): 212–220, pp. 213–4.

that they single out any one reduction as the unique or correct one.

There have been other attempts to argue that we can single out one reduction from the multitude and bless it alone with philosophical significance. Herbert Hochberg, following another theme in Russell, holds that Occam's razor can rid us of a multiplicity of interpretability relations.[6] This suggestion misses the point, however, for at best Occam's razor might be able to adjudicate to which theory we ought to reduce the theory under consideration; given multiply interpretable theories, however, we may assume that the theories involved, and thus the ostensible commitments of those theories, are fixed. Arithmetic, for example, may be interpreted in set theory in a variety of ways, but no ultimate ontological differences separate these reductions; no matter which we choose, we end up with a *prima facie* commitment to the ontology of set theory. Thus Occam's razor fails to shave our multiplicity of interpretations to a single strand, for no interpretation may be considered more or less parsimonious than any other in cases of multiple interpretability.

The only consideration raised with regard to this problem which seems on target is Benacerraf's epistemological one. Focus for a moment on the interpretability relations between arithmetic and set theory. Benacerraf argues that the progression defined by the reduction to be the numbers must be such that the relation "is less than or equal to" is recursive. It is not clear what it means to say that the order relation in an arbitrary progression is recursive, but we can reconstruct what Benacerraf intends by examining the argument. We cannot learn the numbers one by one; we would never be able to go far enough to do very sophisticated calculations. To manage those, we need a rule for constructing arbitrarily large numbers. Furthermore, we want to be able to tell, in a finite time, which of two given numbers is larger. Apparently, then, we must present the set-theoretic progression in such a way that there is a recursive decision procedure for statements of the form "*a* is less than or equal to *b*", where *a* and *b* represent standard names, produced by Post-type rules, for terms of the progression.[7]

6. "Russell's Reduction of Arithmetic to Logic," in E. D. Klemke, ed., *Essays on Bertrand Russell* (Urbana: University of Illinois Press, 1970): 396–415, p. 402; see Russell, "My Mental Development," in Schilpp, p. 14.

7. Benacerraf, *Logicism: Some Considerations*, pp. 164–166; "What Numbers Could Not Be," pp. 51–53. I am indebted to Charles Parsons for recognizing the unclarity of Benacerraf's criterion.

Investigating Benacerraf's suggestion further at this point would take us too far afield. But whether his demand for this additional epistemologically based criterion is legitimate or not, the criterion gives us no way of singling out some reduction as unique. It may allow us to drop some possible candidates from consideration, but a large number of interpretations of arithmetic in set theory still satisfy the added requirement for an algorithm deciding the order relation.

We thus are forced to face the fact that there are many reductions of arithmetic to set theory, no one of which we may pick out, to the exclusion of the others, as the correct reduction. Why is this a difficulty? Why not declare, "the more, the merrier", and bask in the richness of our reductive techniques?

The problem is simply that the reductions disagree. As Benacerraf puts the matter, we are searching for necessary and sufficient conditions for the adequacy of a reduction. In this case, however, many reductions satisfy the conditions formulated thus far, and they conflict with one another. One assigns $\{\{\phi\}\}$ to the number 2, while another assigns $\{\phi, \{\phi\}\}$; there are in fact infinitely many conflicting assignments for each number. Now recall the assumption that, if the number 2 is a set at all, it must be some particular set. It cannot be both $\{\phi, \{\phi\}\}$ and $\{\{\phi\}\}$, or, to make the point more strongly, it cannot be an infinite number of sets at once. If 2 cannot be all these sets, some of the accounts must be wrong; they must fail to meet the proper criteria for the adequacy of a reduction. But we have, in principle, no way of deciding which accounts fail in some way and which might be correct. Thus, Benacerraf concludes, numbers must not be sets after all. Any attempt to reduce numbers to sets, in an ontologically interesting sense, must be doomed. But this is really a more general conclusion: if T is multiply interpretable in T', then T cannot be reducible to T' in any sense that would have implications for ontology.

2. Intertheoretic Identifications

As we have seen, the difficulty arises because the alternative reductions disagree; not on sentences of arithmetic or set theory, of course, for then they would not meet our conditions, but on intertheoretic statements, such as '3 is an element of 17' or '2 = $\{\{\phi\}\}$'. Thus the sort of statement that gives rise to the problem is precisely that which forced Nelson Goodman to abandon extensional identity as a criterion of definitional adequacy in *The Structure of Appearance*.[8] Some of these statements, such as '$\{\phi\}$ is prime', '1 is an element of $\{\{\phi\}\}$', or '$2 = \{\{\phi\}\}$', are peculiar, somewhat offensive to our linguistic intuitions, and have different truth values under different interpretations. Others, though, are even worse. On one interpretation, '$2 = \{\{\phi\}\}$' is true, and on another, '$2 = \{\phi, \{\phi\}\}$' is true, and so, by substitutivity of identicals, we obtain '$\{\{\phi\}\} = \{\phi, \{\phi\}\}$', an absurd conclusion. Benacerraf does not alter the criterion of definitional adequacy, but rather rejects all these intertheoretic statements as meaningless. He focuses his attention on intertheoretic identities, and so shall I, but the other sorts of troublesome sentences must be kept in mind as well.

From the point of view of the classical theory of identity, we face a grave difficulty: '$2 = \{\{\phi\}\}$' and '$2 = \{\phi, \{\phi\}\}$' do indeed entail '$\{\{\phi\}\} = \{\phi, \{\phi\}\}$', and we cannot accept that. Since there is no way of determining which identities we are to accept and which others we should reject, we seem to be forced, on pain of inconsistency, to reject *all* these identity claims.

We might of course argue that there is a way of choosing among the possible interpretations, even though we cannot in principle know what it is. Finding this alternative hopelessly mystical, Benacerraf chooses to hold that none is correct. I shall argue that we have yet another option: all the reductions are formally correct, and we are free to choose to *use* one reduction or another without running into contradictions.

We must consider a complication. Benacerraf does not hold a classical view of identity, but rather a form of relative identity. He believes that an identity statement must be of such a character that some predicate subsumes both terms of the identity and has associated with it a set of identification conditions. Within arithmetic and within set theory, this condition is satisfied: '1 is the same *number* as $S(0)$', '$\{\phi\}$ is the same *set* as $\{\phi, \phi\}$', etc., are legitimate identity statements, because in each case we have such a predicate, and the identification conditions associated with it are clear. But across the boundaries of theories, in intertheoretic identity statements, there are no such predicates, no available identification conditions, which give identity statements a clear sense. We might try to use 'entity', 'mathematical object', or 'abstract object', but these are too broad; as we have seen, these offer no iden-

8. Boston: Reidel, 1951, 1977; see pp. 3–9; see above, chapter two.

tification conditions that allow us to accept some intertheoretic identity claims while rejecting others as false.

Benacerraf concludes that all intertheoretic identity statements are therefore meaningless, owing to lack of relevant identification criteria. They are not false, because no properties distinguish the terms (though he is willing to call them false, presumably because they are "don't cares"). Consequently a philosopher is simply wrong to ask questions about identities across theories, and, by implication, to ask about ontological reduction at all.

The move from the illegitimacy of intertheoretic identities to the meaninglessness of ontological reduction is a quick move in Benacerraf's argument; we find no supporting analysis. But we can reconstruct the outlines of an argument. For Benacerraf, reduction essentially involves identities. What we do in a purportedly ontological reduction is identify the objects of a certain sort with objects or constructions out of objects of another sort; thus we identify numbers with sets, ordered pairs with unordered sets, etc. This, surely, is a fairly intuitively appealing account of reduction. Nevertheless, it is mistaken. I have been arguing that a proper account of reduction is based upon *eliminability*—in particular, upon the eliminability of discourse forcing ostensible commitments upon us—rather than upon identities. Indeed, on my view, reduction does not demonstrate the identity of objects from two different realms, but shows merely that we need not be *committed* to the separation of those realms. Hence, in reducing number theory to set theory, we do not identify numbers with sets, or prove that numbers are *really* sets, but rather show that language ostensibly committing us to numbers as distinct from sets is eliminable. It follows from this that we need not assume that numbers are distinct from sets, for we do not need to mention numbers in our "complete description of the world", to use Russell's phrase. In short, Benacerraf bases his challenge on a concept of ontological reduction fundamentally different from that which I have been advancing. On my view, intertheoretic identifications are not crucial to ontological reduction, as they are on Benacerraf's account. The formal portrait of reduction which I have offered, in fact, does not even require singular terms in the description of the languages involved. Thus, on my approach to reduction, problems involving identities are highly derivative, and what we say about them will have a character quite different from the tenor of Benacerraf's approach.

Benacerraf is somewhat cavalier about the sort of semantic

ambiguity appropriate to intertheoretic sentences; he is willing to call them false, though he prefers to consider them meaningless. They are one or the other, apparently, because no possible circumstances could lead us to decide that they are true or false. There are no methods available, in principle, for choosing among the vast multitude of possible reductions. Interestingly, it is precisely this kind of consideration that has led other philosophers to conclude that certain sentences lack a truth value.[9] Benacerraf's nonchalance seems to be due to his feeling that intertheoretic identities are "don't cares", i.e., that they do not merit serious concern. But this too has been seen as justification for regarding sentences as truth-value-less, rather than meaningless, or, by arbitrary fiat, false.[10]

I shall argue that relative identity relations are meaningful even in intertheoretic contexts, since the interpretation specified by way of the relativization provides adequate identification criteria. If an absolute identity relation can be constructed out of such relative identity relations—and in the following chapter I shall argue that it can—then even absolute identity statements are meaningful across the boundaries of theories. Of course, if we construe them as meaningful, any semantics for them must preserve our ordinary logical laws. As we have seen, the view that all the reductions are correct fails to do this, leading to contradictory conclusions.

We may specify truth conditions for intertheoretic sentences while preserving usual logical laws by assigning all such sentences a value of falsehood, as Benacerraf suggests. Thus, if '$2 = \{\{\phi\}\}$' is false, then '$2 \neq \{\{\phi\}\}$' will be true; so the laws of excluded middle and contradiction are preserved. The defect of this strategy is its artificiality. If no circumstances could lead us to decide that '$2 = \{\{\phi\}\}$' is true (or false), then no circumstances could lead us to discover that '$2 \neq \{\{\phi\}\}$' is false (or true). The asymmetry this strategy introduces into the treatment of the two sentences, then, has no foundation in the philosophical justification for that treatment. The option of construing intertheoretic identities as truth-value-less therefore has the advantage of preserving the

9. Bas van Fraassen, "The Completeness of Free Logic," *Zeitschrift für Mathematische Logik und Grundlagen der Mathematik*, XII (1966): 219–234, p. 219.

10. Peter F. Strawson, "On Referring," in Jay Rosenberg and Charles Travis, eds., *Readings in the Philosophy of Language* (Englewood Cliffs, N.J.: Prentice-Hall, 1971): 175–194; van Fraassen, "Singular Terms, Truth-value Gaps, and Free Logic," *Journal of Philosophy*, LXIII (1966): 481–495.

underlying symmetry between the truth conditions for an atomic sentence and those for its negation.

A final problem with Benacerraf's argument concerns its ambiguity. His argument that '2 = {{φ}}', for example, is meaningless, we can break into two stages. First, if we assume a classical theory of identity, the multiplicity of available reductions, among which we cannot choose, forces us into contradiction. Second, if we attempt to avoid this by invoking the notion of relative identity, we face the problem of having no identification conditions across theories allowing us to specify a relativizing sortal. This seems to alter the argument from one against ontological reduction of multiply reducible theories to one that tells against ontological reduction *per se*:

> ... the philosopher is not satisfied with this limited view of things. He wants to know more and does ask the questions in which the mathematician professes no interest. I agree. He does. And mistakenly so (69).

The status of this move, however, remains unclear. Benacerraf offers no argument to the effect that there are no identification criteria available between theories, or that we need them in the first place; the only argument I can reconstruct is that, since we have no way of choosing among the multiplicity of reductions, there are no sufficiently specific identification conditions. In that case, though, the argument relies on the earlier argument about multiply reducible theories, and justifies no more sweeping conclusion.

I shall begin by focusing on two distinctions Benacerraf makes; a full explication of these distinctions, I shall argue, undermines the conclusions that Benacerraf reaches concerning the plausibility of ontological reduction. (1) According to Benacerraf, identities that cross theoretical boundaries can still have sense if we append to them something like "in Ernie's account", "according to von Neumann's translation", etc. Even then, he says, they are not perspicuous, for numbers are not objects at all; it is better to speak in terms of "correspondences" rather than identities. (Compare Rudolf Carnap's reluctance to speak of identifications in describing the logicist program, because of his repulsion for metaphysical issues.) How is it that identities can make sense, given the specification of a particular interpretation of the one theory into the other? Given Benacerraf's approach to identity in general, it seems that the specification of a particular interpretation must provide identification conditions that allow us to evaluate the statement of identity. '. . . are the same in von Neumann's account', then, amounts to a relative identity relation, with the specification of an interpretation functioning as the predicate mentioned by Benacerraf functions normally in relativized identity statements. (2) Benacerraf distinguishes an assertion of identity from an identification; the latter is acceptable, whereas the former is not, because identifications mean to be nothing other than correspondences, that is, technical ploys that do not pretend to discover what numbers "really" are. Thus, for Benacerraf, the study of interpretability relations is not in itself objectionable, but construing these relations as having ontological significance is. Given Benacerraf's account, however, why are identifications legitimate? How can we go about evaluating their truth value? Once again, given a relative view of identity, these can make sense only if there are some specified identification conditions operative with regard to them. But such identification conditions can come only from some specific interpretation; we have seen that, without such specificity, no identification criteria are available to grant legitimacy to intertheoretic identity statements. Thus, "identifications" are relativized intertheoretic identities, such as '2 = $\{\{\phi\}\}$ (on von Neumann's translation)'; "assertions of identity" are absolute identity statements such as '2 = $\{\{\phi\}\}$'. Benacerraf's two distinctions thus collapse into each other. That is just as well, for clearly much more needs to be said to elucidate the distinctions Benacerraf has in mind.

3. *The Semantics of Intertheoretic Sentences*

In this section I shall present a formal semantics for intertheoretic sentences involved in a multiple reduction. Several *caveats* must be mentioned at the outset. I shall assume that the only problem we need be concerned with is multiple reducibility; the semantics I shall present is thus relative to the theories under consideration and also to the reducibility of the one to the other. This will not always be explicit in the notation, for practical reasons, but should be borne in mind. I intend the semantics to show that we can make sense, formally, of Benacerraf's distinction between "assertions of identity" and "identifications", but that the explication of it leads us to conclusions quite different from those which Benacerraf draws. I shall not discuss in detail in this chapter the relationship between relative and absolute conceptions of identity; the philosophical analysis of that relationship, much of which my semantics will take for granted, is presented in chapter six.

A *theory* is a collection of first-order sentences, closed under logical consequence; a *similarity type* is a collection of individual constants and predicate constants of given -ariness. We will say that a theory T is *of* similarity type s (a fact we will denote by writing '$T(s)$') if and only if the nonlogical symbols of T, other than individual variables, are exactly those which are elements of s.

$I = (f, d)$ is an *interpretation from* s_1 *into* s_2 if and only if d is an s_2-formula with one free variable and f is a recursive function from s_1-predicate constants of n places into s_2-formulas containing n free variables, s_1-individual constants into s_2-individual constants, and individual variables into individual variables such that (where 't', 't_1', etc. represent terms, i.e., either individual constants or individual variables):

(1)	$I(t) = f(t)$ if t is a constant
	$I(t) = f(t) = t$ if t is a variable
(2)	$I(t_1 = t_2) = (I(t_1) = I(t_2))$
(3)	$I(R(t_1, \ldots, t_n)) = f(R)\,(I(t_1), \ldots, I(t_n))$
(4)	$I(-A) = -I(A)$
(5)	$I(A \ \& \ B) = I(A) \ \& \ I(B)$
(6)	$I((x)A) = (x)\,(dx \supset I(A))$

An interpretation I from s_1 into s_2 is an *interpretation of* $T_1(s_1)$ *into* $T_2(s_2)$ if and only if that A is an element of T_1 implies that $I(A)$ is an element of T_2, for any s_1-formula A. $T_1(s_1)$ is *interpretable in* $T_2(s_2)$ *via an interpretation* I *from* s_1 *into* s_2 if and only if I is an interpretation of $T_1(s_1)$ into $T_2(s_2)$. [We will write this '$T_1(s_1) \leq_I T_2(s_2)$'.] Finally, $T_1(s_1)$ is *interpretable in* $T_2(s_2)$ just in case there is an interpretation I such that $T_1(s_1) \leq_I T_2(s_2)$. [This we will write '$T_1(s_1) \leq T_2(s_2)$'.]

A *model structure* $M = (D, \phi)$ of similarity type s is an ordered pair consisting of a nonempty set D (its *domain*) and a total function ϕ (its *function of interpretation*) from the predicates and constants belonging to s into D, such that $\phi(a)$ is an element of D, and $\phi(R^n)$ is a subset of D^n.

An *assignment* α *on a model structure* M is a function from individual variables into D (for $M = (D, \phi)$) such that $\alpha\,(x)$ is an element of D. If α and α' are two assignments on M, that '$\alpha' =_x \alpha$' will mean that α and α' correspond except perhaps on x.

A *denotation function* $d(\alpha, M)$ is a function from terms into D, for $M = \langle D, \phi \rangle$, such that

$$d(\alpha, M) \ (t) = \alpha(t) \text{ if } t \text{ is a constant;}$$
$$= \alpha(t) \text{ if } t \text{ is a variable.}$$

A *valuation function* $V(\alpha, M)$ is a function from formulas into truth values, such that

(1) $V(\alpha, M) \ (Rt_1 \ldots, t_n) = T$ if and only if $<d(\alpha, M) \ (t_1), \ldots, d(\alpha, M) \ (t_n)>$ is an element of $\phi(R)$;

(2) $V(\alpha, M) \ (t_1 = t_2) = T$ if and only if $d(\alpha, m) \ (t_1) = d(\alpha, M) \ (t_2)$;

(3) $V(\alpha, M) \ (-A) = T$ if and only if $V(\alpha, M) \ (A) = F$;

(4) $V(\alpha, M) \ (A \ \& \ B) = T$ if and only if $V(\alpha, M) \ (A) = V(\alpha, M) \ (B) = T$;

(5) $V(\alpha, M) \ ((x)A) = T$ if and only if $V(\alpha', M) \ (A) = T$ for every α' such that $\alpha' = {}_x\alpha$.

This gives us a total function from formulas into the set of truth values, namely $\{T, F\}$. But we are interested only in statements, that is, in formulas with no free variables, for we do not want assignments to free variables to make a real difference in the semantics. To obtain a valuation for sentences, we need only notice that, if α and α' are two assignments that agree on all the free variables in a formula A, then $V(\alpha, M)$ assigns the same truth value to A as $V(\alpha', M)$ does. Thus, if A has no free variables, the valuations agree vacuously. As a result, we can define a sentence valuation $V(M)$:

$$V(M) = V(\alpha, M) \text{ for any (or all) } \alpha$$

A sentence valuation $V(M)$ gives us a definition of truth in a model structure.

We face, however, two problems. First, we are interested not in all model structures of a language, but only in those which model a theory T and which further, in some sense to be made precise, satisfy the "structure" of an interpretation I. Thus we want to speak of the models that somehow correspond to, say, the von Neumann translation of arithmetic into set theory, as opposed to the models corresponding to the Zermelo translation. Second, we are interested in determining not merely truth values for a model structure, even a structure of a special sort, but truth values *over* model structures, that is, truth values *simpliciter*. Thus we do not want to relativize our semantics for intertheoretic statements to individual models; we want a semantics for those sentences considered in themselves. Of course, this aim cannot be fully achieved here; the truth values our semantics yields are not relative to model structures, but they are relative to other things.

Let us consider the first problem: we are interested in the case where we have two theories such that one of them, say $T_1(s_1)$, can be interpreted in the other, say $T_2(s_2)$, in more than one way, i.e., via at least two distinct interpretations I and I'. Further, we want a unified semantics for these theories. We will therefore consider a larger theory T^* in the similarity type $(s_1 \cup s_2)$ which includes at least all the theorems of T_1 and T_2. For the sake of simplicity, we will assume that s_1 and s_2 are disjoint, as Tarski does, though this represents no essential limitation.

A model structure $M = \langle D, \phi \rangle$ *is a model of a theory* $T(s)$ if and only if, for every s-formula A, if A is an element of T, then M satisfies A.

A model structure $M = \langle D, \phi \rangle$ in $(s_1 \cup s_2)$ *conforms to* an interpretation $I = \langle f, d \rangle$ from $T_1(s_1)$ into $T_2(s_2)$ if and only if: (1) M is a model of both T_1 and T_2; (2) $\phi(a) = \phi(I(a))$ for any individual constant a in s_1; (3) $\phi(R^n) = \phi(f(R^n))$ for any n-ary predicate R^n in s_1.

Since we already understand what a valuation function on a model is, we can readily understand a valuation function on a model conforming to some interpretation I. To show that such a valuation function exists for an I such that $T_1 \leq_I T_2$, then, it is necessary and sufficient to show that there is a model structure M that conforms to I. This, in turn, we can demonstrate by showing that there is a model satisfying both T_1 and T_2, which is true so long as T_1 and T_2 are compatible theories. But, as we have shown in chapter four, this is tantamount to the assumption that T_2 is consistent. If T_2 is not consistent, then we can regard the resulting valuation as trivial.

A valuation relative to a model conforming to some interpretation I has some important semantical properties. In particular, such a valuation is bivalent; every closed formula is assigned a truth value. The next valuation function we will examine does not have this property.

We may construct the *valuation conforming to an interpretation* I, such that $T_1 \leq_I T_2$, as follows:

$V(I)(A) = $ T if and only if $V(M)(A) = $ T for every model M conforming to I of T_1 into T_2;

$V(I)(A) = F$ if and only if $V(M)(A) = F$ for every model M conforming of I to T_1 into T_2;

$V^*(A)$ is undefined otherwise.

Although the valuation function relative to a model structure conforming to an interpretation is a total function, which assigns a value to every closed formula and thus yields a bivalent semantics, the valuation conforming to an interpretation is no longer total; for some formulas, the value assigned by the function will be undefined. Such formulas we will refer to as *truth-value-less* on that valuation. Further, it is clear that so long as incomplete theories are being considered (and most of the theories of any interest in this context are incomplete), there will be some formulas that do not receive truth values on such a valuation.

The valuation function relative to an interpretation gives us a solution to the first problem; we now have a valuation that is intimately linked with the theories under consideration and the structure of the interpretation relating them. But, since we are interested in multiply reducible theories, we must also focus on the second problem, which insists that we want, not just truth values relative to an interpretation I, but truth values *simpliciter*. To solve this problem, we use the strategy that allows a move from valuations relative to a model conforming to an interpretation to valuations simply relative to interpretations. In that case, we quantified over models, in effect binding the variable that made the function relative to models as well as interpretations. Similarly, we want to remove the dependence of the valuation function on the particular interpretation involved; this we can accomplish by quantifying over interpretations, thus binding the variable I.

Finally, then, we construct a supervaluation V^*. Let $T_1(s_1)$ and $T_2(s_2)$ be two theories as described above, and let $J = \{I: T_1 \leq {}_I T_2\}$. Assume that J contains at least two elements. Then we can define:

$V^*(A) = T$ if and only if $V(I)(A) = T$ for all I in J;

$V^*(A) = F$ if and only if $V(I)(A) = F$ for all I in J;

$V^*(A)$ is undefined otherwise.

Once again, V^* is a partial function; so some formulas (namely, those on which the various interpretations disagree) will turn out to be truth-value-less on this valuation.

To see what effect this has on our original difficulty, re-member the sentences that were particularly troublesome to Benacerraf and Goodman: sentences such as '3 is an element of 17', '2 = $\{\{\phi\}\}$', '2 = $\{\phi, \{\phi\}\}$', and so on. Where arithme-tic is the theory represented by T_1 and set theory that repre-sented by T_2, V^* will assign no truth value to these sentences, for they are sentences on which the variety of interpretations disagree. Nevertheless, they are meaningful sentences on our semantics, even if they are only dubiously useful, for they do have truth conditions, and logical laws are preserved over them. Thus '2 = $\{\phi, \{\phi\}\} \vee 2 \neq \{\phi, \{\phi\}\}$' will come out true under the supervaluation, for this holds in every interpreta-tion; all interpretations of arithmetic in set theory agree on this and on other excluded-middle instances, so the super-valuation assigns truth to all of them. Thus V^* preserves the validity of the law of excluded middle, even though it is not bivalent.[11]

The seemingly contradictory conclusions that Benacerraf attempts to draw from sentences such as '2 = $\{\{\phi\}\}$' and '2 = $\{\phi, \{\phi\}\}$', namely, in this instance, '$\{\{\phi\}\} = \{\phi\}\}$', do not follow on my account. The original identity statements are not true now, but truth-value-less; that substitution should give us absurd consequences, then, is not surprising, for the identity claims justifying the substitutions are not true on this semantics. But an even stronger point may be made. The sentence '2 = $\{\{\phi\}\}$ & 2 = $\{\phi, \{\phi\}\}$' comes out false on the present account, for no interpretation assigns two differ-ent sets to the number 2. All the interpretations agree in preserving the law of contradiction; so the above sentence, which could certainly have very damaging consequences, is assigned falsehood by the semantics. As a result, there is no danger that we will be driven, on pain of inconsistency, to reject identity claims or other intertheoretic statements; the semantics preserves noncontradiction.

Though the supervaluation V^* gives us a semantics for absolute identity statements in an intertheoretic context, we have also provided a natural representation of relative iden-tity statements in this semantics. Recall the valuation func-tion conforming to an interpretation, $V(I)$. Since we are es-pecially interested in the treatment given identity statements by these valuations, let us abbreviate '$V(I)$ $(t_1 = t_2) = \mathrm{T}$' as

11. See van Fraassen, "The Completeness of Free Logic," p. 223. The "state-models" of van Fraassen's semantics have the property that, though they are not bivalent, every statement of the form '$A \vee -A$' is true on every state-model.

simply '$t_1 = {}_I t_2$', to be read as "t_1 is identical with t_2 relative to interpretation I" or, to give this a more Geachian flavor, "t_1 is the same I-object as t_2." A specific interpretation makes such sentences meaningful, for it does provide identification conditions; we have seen that Benacerraf admits as much by granting the legitimacy of identifications, as opposed to assertions of identity. We cannot know which set to single out as identical with the number 1, say, in an absolute sense, but, given a specific interpretation of arithmetic in set theory, it is utterly clear which set is to be assigned to each number. Thus there are no grounds for failing to hold that each interpretation provides its own set of identification conditions. The expression of this in Geach's idiom, saying that we have legitimate sortals 'von-Neumann-object', 'Zermelo-object', etc., is perhaps misleading; we should construe these sortals as indicating that each of the interpretations referred to by the sortals provides adequate identification conditions for the clarification of the truth values of the identities between sets and numbers.

That these relations, symbolized by '$= {}_I$', are relative identity relations in the sense of Geach or Benacerraf is easy to see: they are equivalence relations, and license substitutions within a limited field, which is specified by I.[12]

We can thus, on this semantics, distinguish clearly between relative and absolute identity relations in intertheoretic contexts; we can spell out the links between them in terms of the supervaluational semantics of V^*. We thus have a precise parsing of Benacerraf's distinction between identifications and assertions of identity. By an identification, he means a correlation, something like "$2 = \{\{\phi\}\}$' (on von Neumann's account)"; this we represent in the semantics by a sentence of the form '$t_1 = {}_I t_2$'. An assertion of identity, on the other

---

12. The proof of this assertion is fairly trivial. That they are equivalence relations is easy to verify. To see that they license substitutions within limited contexts, assume that $t = {}_I t'$. Then $V(M) (t = t') = T$ for every model M conforming to I. But then $d(\alpha, M) (t) = d(\alpha, M) (t')$ in each of these models. If 't' and 't'' are substitutable *salva veritate* in atomic sentences, they can be substituted *salva veritate* in any extensional context. And atomic sentences will be of two forms: identity statements, such as '$t = t''$', or relational formulas, '$Rt_1, \ldots, t_n$'. The identity case is trivial; a relational formula is true on a model just in case $<d (\alpha, M) (t_1), \ldots, d(\alpha, M) (t_n)>$ is an element of $\phi (R)$. But, since the substitution of 't' for 't'' or vice versa does not change the value of the denotation function at the appropriate place in this n-tuple, the valuation function will assign the same truth value in both cases. Notice, however, that this occurs only within a limited field, namely, in those models conforming to I.

hand, is something like '2 = {{ϕ}}', not relativized to some particular interpretation but intended *tout court*. These we represent in the semantics by absolute identity statements to which the supervaluation V^* sometimes assigns truth values.

Benacerraf concludes "What Numbers Could Not Be" by claiming that numbers are places in a sequence, not objects; of course, then, they are not sets or whatever else one might take them to be. Similarly Gilbert Harman has argued in several papers that numbers are functions in a sequence, relating some particular object to some place in a sequence. Both Harman and Benacerraf, then, stress that the *roles* of number words in the appropriate sequences tell us all we need to know about what numbers are.[13] Though I disagree with many of the details of Benacerraf's treatment, I concur in this final judgment.

If we take seriously the contention that numbers are, as it were, linguistic roles which may be played by a variety of bits of language, we end up with something very much like my semantics, and no problems such as those envisioned by Benacerraf arise. If '2 = {{ϕ}}' and '2 = {ϕ, {ϕ}}' have, roughly, the form

'2' is a ·{{ϕ}}·

'2' is a ·{ϕ, }ϕ}}·

then they are similar to the sentences "'rot' is a ·decay·" and "'rot' is a ·red·"; we may conclude either that 'rot' is ambiguous or that some reference to specific languages and translation manuals is missing. Thus we are likely to prefer "'rot' is a ·decay· (in English)" and "'rot' is a ·red· (in German)", which are hardly contradictory. But these have the same form as

'2' is a ·{{ϕ}}· (in von Neumann's translation)

'2' is a ·{ϕ, {ϕ}}· (in Zermelo's translation)

which correspond to relativized identity statements and which are not contradictory either.[14]

---

13. Benacerraf, pp. 69ff; Gilbert H. Harman, "A Nonessential Property," *Journal of Philosophy*, LXVII (1970): 183–185; "Identifying Numbers," *Analysis*, XXXV (1974): 12.

14. For some background concerning the dot-quoting device, see Wilfrid Sellars, "Abstract Entities," *Review of Metaphysics*, XVI (1963): 229–269; *Naturalism and Ontology* (Reseda, Calif.: Ridgeview, 1979) pp. 102–131.

The relativizing interpretations that I recognize in my semantics are conventional in spirit; given some particular interpretation or translation manual, reference to a number can be avoided in favor of reference to a set. The eliminability is philosophically significant, but which interpretation we use to do the actual eliminating is a matter of convention. This appeal to convention might make little sense with regard to physical theories, which commit us to full-blooded, physical objects; the lesson to be learned, then, is that the analogy between physical and abstract objects is a loose analogy. To spell it out in detail would require a full analysis of interpretability relations as relations between linguistic roles in different theories, but that is a task for another time.

6 Relative Identity Reconsidered

Peter Geach has launched an all-out attack on the classical theory of identity, by claiming that there is no single relation of identity, of being "the same", but only relations of relative identity, of being "the same F", where 'F' represents some substantival term.[1] Geach's arguments for his position have stirred up quite a controversy, and frequently (and rightly, I think) have been rejected. I shall consider, however, an argument for relative identity which at best has appeared implicitly in his writings, and I shall claim that, though this argument falls short of establishing Geach's thesis, it nevertheless forces the classical identity theorist to make some important concessions. I shall attempt to show that we can grant much to the relative-identity advocate and still construct the classical logic of identity statements, or a very close approximation to it. The alterations we are forced to make in the course of the construction reveal an element of truth in Geach's position.

1. The Relative-identity Thesis

Except where we supply a substantival term, either explicitly or contextually, Geach says, statements of identity are "vague expressions of a half-formed thought", "have no sense" and "no significance."[2] Geach's relative-identity thesis thus states that the specification of a substantival is a condition for the meaningfulness of any claim involving identity. We ought, therefore, to be perspicuous, never write '$a = b$', but rather '$a =_F b$', which should be understood as short for 'a is the same F as b'.

What sort of relations are relative identity relations? They are not to be analyzed in terms of absolute identity, clearly, but are to be taken as primitive. What properties do they

---

1. See "Identity," *Review of Metaphysics*, XXI (1967/8): 3–12; "A Reply," *Review of Metaphysics*, XXII (1969): 556–559; *Mental Acts* (New York: Humanities Press, 1957); *Reference and Generality* (Ithaca, N.Y.: Cornell, 1968); "Ontological Relativity and Relative Identity," in Milton K. Munitz, ed., *Logic and Ontology* (New York: NYU Press, 1973): 287–302. Parenthetical page references to Geach will be to "Identity" unless noted otherwise.

2. "Identity," p. 3; *Reference and Generality*, p. 39; *Mental Acts*, p. 69.

have? How do we distinguish possible candidates for relative identity relations?

Geach answers that relative identity relations are *I-predicables*: an *I*-predicable in a theory *T* is a two-place predicate *P* in *T* which satisfies the schema

$$Fa \equiv (\exists x)\,(Fx \;\&\; Pxa)$$

for all expressions *F* constructible in *T* (4). Identity, understood relatively, amounts to indiscernibility within a given theory. Just as there is no absolute identity, so there is no absolute indiscernibility, but only indiscernibility relative to a set of descriptive resources.[3] It follows from the satisfaction of the above schema that relations of relative identity are equivalence relations and that they permit substitutions of relative identicals, but only within the confines of the theory with respect to which they are indiscernible.

To illustrate the point, imagine two theories *T* and *T'*, where *T* is a subtheory of *T'* and where *T'* contains some predicate *G* that allows us to distinguish between objects indistinguishable relative to the ideology of *T*. Suppose, for example, that *T* is a very simple physical theory that does not allow us to distinguish (within *T*) between objects having the same mass. Let us say that *T'* contains *T*, but also a predicate *G* permitting us to distinguish objects having distinct spatial locations, and that *T* contains a predicate *P* satisfying Geach's schema characterizing *I*-predicables. In considering these theories, we have two options: we might interpret *P* as absolute identity in *T*, but interpret the same predicate as merely an equivalence relation in *T'* (for example, 'has the same mass as'). Or we might treat *P* as a relation of relative identity in both theories; Geach favors this option. Why?

2. The Argument from the Possibility of Revision

I shall consider an argument meaning to show that we ought to favor this option as well; I shall call it the *argument from the possibility of revision*. Contemplate the situation involving *T* and *T'* from the perspective of an individual who holds *T* to be true; *T'*, unbeknownst to him, let us say, is a bigger and better theory than *T* in the sense that what *T'* adds to *T* is true. Now, for Geach, relative identity is really indiscernibility relative to a set of descriptive and discriminative resources (not all of which need to be lexical); so the shift

3. Geach, "Ontological Relativity and Relative Identity," p. 298.

from T to T' would require an increase in these resources. If our hypothetical theory holder were to accept T', he would admit that what he thought was an object in T was really a multiplicity under the stronger microscope provided by the discriminative resources of T'.

Now, the argument goes, we can never be in a position to know that our set of discriminative resources cannot be made stronger in just this way, by a move to a stronger theory that leads us to see previously indiscriminable objects as in fact distinct. We never, in other words, reach a position where our theories are not open to revision. Furthermore, our theories lie open to revision not merely in the sense that we might have a mistake lurking somewhere within them, but in the sense that, though our theories are correct as far as they go, they can be correctly supplemented so that what appeared as an object before will now seem to be a multiplicity. If we could reach a position where our theories were immune from this sort of revision, then we would be justified in adopting a classical theory of identity, for we could claim to have had access to all the relevant F's before asserting '$a = b$' on the grounds that, for any constructible expression F with one free variable, $Fa \equiv Fb$. But we can never achieve this state of affairs; there is no analogue to a completeness proof when we speak in terms of "truths about the world." We therefore are forced to adopt a theory which holds that identity is relative, admitting that we assert any identity statement based only upon an examination of a limited number of predicates. As Robert Kraut puts it, "today's identities are tomorrow's mere qualitative similarities."[4]

The argument, as it stands, is not fully convincing; perhaps one's feeling of being moved by it is proportional to one's fear of intellectual embarrassment. The argument from the possibility of revision in this form fails to distinguish identity claims from any other assertions we make about the world. Suppose, for example, we evaluate the assertion that Mt. Everest is the highest mountain on earth. An increase in information might lead us to recant this claim; no matter how hard or how long we search, we can never be in a position to assert, without any fear of possible revision, of any mountain that *it* is the highest. Such a claim might have the form, say, "There is no mountain on earth having a height greater than

4. *Objects* (Ph.D. dissertation, University of Pittsburgh, 1976), p. 52. Parenthetical page references to Kraut will be to this work, unless otherwise noted. See also his "Indiscernibility and Ontology," *Synthese*, XLIV (1980): 113–135.

that of Mt. X," or something quite similar. This is a negative existential sentence, however, and it is well known that sentences of this form cannot be verified conclusively, simply because of their logical structure. Are we forced, then, to assert only that Mt. Everest is the highest mountain, relative to the information we now possess? In brief, *all* our assertions about the world suffer from the ineluctable possibility of revision. Thus, if it is the possibility of revision alone which leads us to adopt relative identity, we ought to relativize every statement to sets of discriminative resources, bits of information, evidential data, etc.; virtually all our claims should then be construed as meaningless in their usual forms, as "vague expressions of half-formed thoughts." How can we single out identity claims?

I do not know how Geach might respond to this question, for he never explicitly presents the argument from the possibility of revision. Robert Kraut deserves credit for articulating the argument in his dissertation, *Objects*, and might well argue as follows. Though it is true that we can never assert with absolute certainty that Mt. Everest is the highest mountain on earth, this is, in essence, an epistemological point. We have no reasonable doubt that there is a highest mountain, or at least some mountains than which none are higher, out there, whether Everest is the right one or not; the difficulty pertains to our knowing which, without any fear that we might later discover a higher one. Identity statements, however, are not analogous. It is not simply that we cannot know them with certainty, but that there are no objects clearly individuated out there to be countenanced as ontologically fundamental or to be recognized as providing some ground for an absolute identity relation. We cannot make identity assertions with certainty, then, because assertions of absolute identity are radically misguided. There is a highest mountain, whether we know what it is or not, but there is no absolute identity for us to know anything about, because there are no most basic objects. No totality of predicates, no perfect theory or set of discriminative resources from which to make claims of absolute identity exists (57ff).

Still, this does not complete a portrait of the situation. Perhaps looking for absolute identity is not quite like looking for the highest mountain, but there is an ambiguity about what it *is* like. It may be that we are trying to achieve something which, though unachievable, can be approximated with increasing precision; looking for absolute identity might be, then, like looking for the number closest to zero. In contrast, it may be that our search depends for its significance upon the task on which we embark and upon our aims, goals, and purposes. Thus looking for absolute identity might be like looking for the right number to divide by; the question, Is *a* identical with *b*? may then have no sense at all without some reference to our purposes in asking the question. Kraut, Quine, and Dummett see the relative-identity theorist as committed to the latter alternative, as evoking the picture of "an amorphous lump of reality, in itself not articulated into distinct objects,"[5] of "a seething, shimmering mass or mess devoid of intrisic individuation."[6] How we individuate the lump of reality depends on what we want to do; we typically vary our lexical, or better, discriminative spectacles according to the job at hand.[7] Thus there is no point in seeking an absolute identity relation, or, what amounts to the same thing, a privileged way of carving up the world into objects; that is like searching for the proper purpose, as if there could be such a thing, for naturally the way we carve up the world will depend on our purposes at the moment. If I am trying to match paint colors, I may well carve up the world into colors, not bothering with any finer distinctions; if I am a particle physicist looking for a new subatomic particle, I will split up the universe very finely indeed.

Neither Kraut nor Dummett appears to notice that we are not forced to this portrait of reality, even if we refuse to grant the analogy between identity statements and the rest of our uncertain assertions about the world. That denial is just as compatible with a picture of the world as an infinitely complex mass which, in contrast to having no form at all, has an infinitely complicated form. We can reasonably imagine, in other words, that *I*-predicables, or sets of discriminative resources, or individuating spectacles, might be of such a character that we can order them as more or less precise, more or less perspicuous. Might we then order objects as more or less ontologically basic, even though the search for the most ontologically basic objects may be hopeless? The picture I am trying to paint bears a similarity to that Kripke portrays in his semantics for intuitionistic logic. Conceive of an infinite series of levels, each of which represents a stage in the advance of knowledge. There is no ultimate level, so there is no

5. Michael Dummett, *Frege: Philosophy of Language* (London: Harper & Row, 1973), p. 548.

6. W. V. Quine, "Identity," mimeographed; quoted in Kraut, p. 46.

7. Kraut, pp. 59, 66.

point at which one can look back and have no fear of the possibility of the revision of present theories; nevertheless there is a sense in which knowledge gets better and better, in which such a state of affairs is asymptotically approximated. We may think of the hypothetical move from T to T', with which our story began, as typifying the transition from one such level to another.

If this picture of reality is fairly coherent, then we can see that an ambiguity mars the conclusion of the argument from the possibility of revision. Further, the ambiguity has great significance for the relative-identity theorist, for the classical theorist may make some philosophical moves that parallel those made by Quine concerning the legitimacy of questions of ontology. If we ask, Is a identical with b?, the relative-identity theorist claims that he cannot understand the question. If we revise our query and ask, Is a identical with b, relative to the best set of discriminative resources?, he can deny that such an animal exists. But if we ask, Is a identical with b, relative to the best set of discriminative resources available to us now?, either he has to tell us, or he has to deny that there is any way of judging when one pair of discriminative lenses is better than another, apart from some reference to goals or purposes.

Now this alternative does make a good deal of sense. As Kraut takes pains to observe, we do switch our discriminative spectacles as our purposes shift. If I am trying to match paint colors, then the best lenses I can adopt are "colorese" lenses that ignore finer distinctions than those based on color; if I try using "paper-thickness" lenses, I will surely be a disaster as an interior decorator. Similarly, in trying to identify governmental posts I may adopt "official personage" lenses, and if I try using my "person" lenses instead, I am certain to boggle at presidents and commanders-in-chief, not to mention double-dippers.

But though there is a good deal of truth to this alternative, it fails to take into account a crucial fact. As philosophers, we are not asking these questions about identity idly, but with a purpose of our own already at hand. Just what this purpose is, of course, is a matter of considerable and probably perpetual dispute. But it seems fair in the present context to say that the philosopher's purpose, at least qua metaphysician, is to achieve as complete and as accurate an understanding of the world as possible. Thus we do not ask for the best set of discriminative resources, with no particular goals and purposes in mind; we ask for the most accurate and complete set of discriminative resources, and thus "the best" comes with its own built-in, already specified sense, simply because a philosopher qua philosopher is asking the question. It is therefore crucial that the relative-identity theorist who wants to reject even the most watered-down of our questions not accept the accurate and complete representation of the world as a legitimate purpose. For even if we admit that no set of discriminative resources is perfectly complete and perspicuous, so long as we may roughly order sets of discriminative spectacles as more or less complete and accurate, absolute identity has its foot in the door. The talk of the strength of discriminative resources, by Geach and Kraut, for example, suggests that we might construct such an ordering. If we identify, as do both Geach and Kraut, a set of discriminative resources with an ideology or a set of predicates in a language (for we can assign lexical correlates to nonlexical resources), then we can say that a theory T has a stronger set of discriminative resources than a theory T' if and only if the ideology of T' is a proper subset of the ideology of T. Or we might want to strengthen this notion and say that T has a stronger set of discriminative resources than T' if and only if the ideology of T' is a proper subset of the ideology of T and there is some predicate F in both T and T' such that F is an I-predicable in T' but an equivalence relation, not an I-predicable, in T. Both these notions give us an ordering relation that is irreflexive, symmetric, and transitive, though obviously not connected: we need not rank "colorese" and "paper-thickness-ese" vis-à-vis each other. But we might well want to extend this notion nevertheless, so that, for example, the manifest and scientific frameworks can be compared even though one does not contain the other. It follows that our question concerning the most accurate and complete set of discriminative resources may have no unique answer, but in that case we can construct a unique set, simply by taking the union of the ideologies of those which are such that no theory has a stronger set of discriminative resources than they do, and treating that union as the unique set.

The moral that I wish to draw from this discussion is twofold: (1) At best, the argument from the possibility of revision supports relativity to a language or theory—*language relativism*, I shall say—rather than Geach's relativism to a substantival. Kraut identifies these, but Geach directly denies the equivalence, insisting that he does not even understand language relativism.[8] But just as Geach insists that there are only relations of the form '$a = {}_F b$', where 'F' represents some substantival, language relativism insists that there are only relations of the form '$a = {}_L b$', where 'L' represents a language, or more particularly, a set of predicates, i.e., an ideology or set of descriptive resources.

In fact, the thesis of language relativism is weaker than Geach's relativity to a substantival. Kraut's identification of these two depends on his claim that, given any language or, better, discriminative framework, one can find a covering sortal that will fulfill the function of Geach's substantivals: "For any framework F we can invoke a sortal, say S, which *somehow* 'corresponds' to that framework" (50). The sortal is a correlate of the ideology of a given theory; that a and b are indiscernible relative to the ideology of T is the truth condition for '$a = {}_{S_T} b$', where 'S_T' denotes the sortal correlated with the ideology of T (74, 86). Sometimes this is surely true. If we speak a language, or use a theory, which does not discriminate between objects having the same color, then clearly 'color' will do as such a substantival; if we do not distinguish between objects except insofar as they fulfill different positions in the United States government, then 'official personage' may serve as an adequate covering sortal. But what of the set of discriminative resources that consists of the set of predicates found in the unabridged English dictionary? Or what about the ideology of the whole of mathematics? Do we use 'English-object'? 'Mathematical-object'? Obviously these terms will not perform the work the Geachian rubric requires of them, for they are far too broad to carry with them any clear identification criteria. Thus Kraut's identification, though it seems to hold for very simple frameworks, fails when the framework becomes sophisticated enough that, in some case where '$a = {}_F b$ & $a \neq {}_G b$' turns out to be true, 'F' and 'G' are both in the ideology of the framework. Thus language relativism does not entail substantival relativism; we may specify a language or theory without specifying a substantival that might be acceptable to Geach. It is probably true, however, that substantival relativism implies language relativism. For any substantival providing identification conditions for some identity statement, we can construct a simple language or theory, though probably not a unique one, for which that substantival is an I-predicable, or allows us to characterize a

8. See Kraut, pp. 50, 77; Fred Feldman, "Geach and Relative Identity," *Review of Metaphysics*, XXII (1969): 547–555, p. 554; Geach, "A Reply," p. 559.

related I-predicable. Hence, even if the argument justifies Kraut's language relativism, it need not support Geach's stronger form of relativism.

(2) Though it may be that relativity to some discriminative framework is an important thing to stress philosophically, the possibility of revision in itself does not force us to the conclusion that absolute identity claims are meaningless. At worst, the argument from the possibility of revision seems to show that we can make such claims only from the best resources available, while admitting not only the possibility but the inevitability of revision. But this does not place identity statements in a position different from that occupied by most theoretical assertions of natural science.

3. *The Logic of Identity*

If we accept the thesis that identity is relative, whether to a substantival or to a language, we face the problem of reconstructing the logic of identity. Classical identity theory is clearly committed to the view that statements of absolute identity are meaningful. Nevertheless, neither Geach nor any of the other supporters of relative identity has offered a satisfying reconstruction; few, in fact, have even attempted the task. I shall consider how we might go about reconstructing identity theory, and argue that, even if some version of relative identity theory is accepted, we can construct a close approximation to the classical theory of identity to demonstrate that statements of absolute identity can be construed as meaningful.

Crucial to the logic of identity is Leibniz's law: $a = b$ if and only if $(F)(Fa \equiv Fb)$. Geach's relative-identity thesis clearly contradicts this principle; indeed, it is incompatible even with the claim that Leibniz's law is meaningful. Geach does not find the law so deserving of uncritical assent as do some of his opponents, and even offers a counterexample: "an ordered pair of integers [e.g., (2, 3)] can be the same rational number as another ordered pair [e.g., (4, 6)] and yet not the same ordered pair."[9] Now John Perry has claimed that all sorts of absurdities follow from Geach's rejection of Leibniz's law, but, as Kraut has indicated, he is simply wrong. We have already noted that relative identity relations are equivalence relations and license substitutions, but only within the context of theories or languages for which they remain I-

---

9. In a letter to Leslie Stevenson, quoted in Stevenson, "Relative Identity and Leibniz's Law," *Philosophical Quarterly,* XXII (1972): 155–158, p. 155.

predicables. Perry's arguments rely on applying substitutions outside of those contexts.[10]

But even if it is not absurd to reject Leibniz's law, what is to take its place? How can we reconstruct the logic of identity statements? Here Geach himself is virtually silent, but others have suggested two candidates as replacements for Leibniz's law.

First, Kraut has offered:

> '$a = b$' is true in L if and only if, for every formula $A(x)$ with one free variable in L, '$A(a) \equiv A(b)$' is true in L

as a replacement; '$a =_F b$' then licenses substitutions only in contexts mobilizing the same discriminative resources as that language or theory for which F is the covering sortal. We have seen that the notion of a covering sortal is not terribly clear; though, given F, we can find a theory for which it is the covering sortal, there is no reason to assume that there is any unique such theory. Furthermore, since we run into trouble in trying to find a covering sortal for a sufficiently complicated theory, the move from Kraut's suggested replacement to conclusions concerning the substitutability of terms relatively identified is problematic.

Eddy Zemach has offered:

> $a =_F b$ if and only if, for some theory T in which F is a sortal, and for every formula $A(x)$ with one free variable in the language of T, 'Fa', 'Fb', and '$A(a) \equiv A(b)$' are theorems of T.[11]

More simply, Zemach stipulates that a is the same F as b just in case a and b are indiscernible in a theory in which both are F's. But this does not seem adequate, for surely we want,

10. See "The Same F," *Philosophical Review*, LXXIX (1970): 181–200; Kraut, pp. 50, 83; Eddy Zemach, "In Defense of Relative Identity," *Philosophical Studies*, XXVI (1974): 207–218, p. 217.

11. Zemach, p. 217. In fact this is a reformed version of Zemach's suggestion, that "$a =_F b$ if and only if $(\exists t) T (Fa \ \& \ Fb \ \& \ SF \ \& \ (g)(ga \equiv gb), t)$", which he would have us read, "a is the same F as b if and only if there is some theory t in which it is true that a is F, that b is F, that F is a sortal property, and that for every property g in t, a is g if and only if b is g." I owe thanks to Charles Parsons for pointing out the confusion between first- and second-order languages in this and in Kraut's earlier offering. Zemach also seems to confuse theoremhood and truth; theorems *of* a theory and theorems *about* a theory; and predicates or formulas and properties. Finally, he seems to require that theory t contain the predicate 'is a sortal'.

at least, something like "for some *true* theory *T*." After all, the theory I appeal to in support of my claim that this chair is the same piece of furniture as that table might be patently absurd; it may be that 'There is only one piece of furniture' is a theorem, perhaps because all terms allowing for discrimination of spatial location, size, etc., are lacking. We might try to correct this by making Zemach's truth condition a condition for the truth of '$a =_F b$' in a specified theory T, that is, for 'a is the same F as b in T', by dropping the phrase 'for some theory T in which'. This, however, gives us theory relativism, which appears to be distinct from both Geach's substantival relativism and Kraut's language relativism. The repair of Zemach's suggestion thus leads to relativity both to a substantival and to a theory in which it appears, and tells us nothing about the truth value of a relative identity claim taken by itself, independent of some particular theory.

Intuitively, what seems closer to the spirit of Geach's relativism is the condition:

'$a =_F b$' is true if and only if Fa and Fb, where F is a sortal, and, for any F-predicate Q_F, $Q_F(a) \equiv Q_F(b)$.

The F-predicates, the Q_F's, are those predicates which are relevant to the individuation and identification of F's. What such predicates are, of course, for each substantival, is not easy to indicate. But the difficulty is by no means unique to this approach and, in fact, gives problems such as that of personal identity their bite. Kraut wants '$a =_F b$' to have as a truth condition that a and b are indistinguishable relative to the set of discriminative resources, or the ideology, relevant to identifying F's: the language, if there is a unique language, having F as a covering sortal. In the terms of my suggestion, the elements of this set are simply the Q_F's. In addition, Geach makes it clear that he wants 'a is the same F as b' to imply that a and b are F's; my truth condition takes this into account (as does Zemach's), though Kraut's does not. On Kraut's parsing, '$a =_F b$' implies only '$Fa \equiv Fb$', rather than 'Fa & Fb', which Geach's intentions seem to demand.

This is not a trivial observation; in fact it cuts to the heart of the distinction between Geach's relativity to a substantival and Kraut's relativity to a language or discriminative framework. Why does Geach, after all, want 'a is the same F as b' to imply that a and b are F's? The cases he has in mind are cases such as 'The President of the United States is the same person as the Commander-in-Chief', 'this word is the same type-word as that', etc.; each fulfills the rubric. The President and the Commander-in-Chief are both persons, and the two words in question are both type-words (neglecting the unclarity surrounding Geach's explanation of what "type-words" are). Kraut, in contrast, has some very different cases in mind. 'The chair is the same color as the table', 'I am the same height as my brother', and 'This inscription is the same length as that one' all make perfect sense given Kraut's paradigm. It is legitimate to say that the chair and the table are indiscriminable relative to the colorese framework (i.e., the framework in which all items of the same color are indiscernible), or that my brother and I are indiscriminable relative to a framework that does not distinguish things of the same height. Similarly, we can say that two inscriptions are indiscernible relative to a set of discriminative resources which is so impoverished that no two things of the same length can be distinguished. Nevertheless, the pieces of furniture are not colors, my brother and I are not heights, and the inscriptions are not lengths. Thus, if we mean to treat examples of this kind, as Kraut clearly does, we will naturally reject the entailment Geach insists upon in his substantival relativism.

From the point of view of the substantival relativist, Kraut is constructing his theory a bit too broadly. Geach no doubt did not have terms such as 'color' in mind as substantivals; he would prefer to say 'The chair is *of* the same color as the table' or 'The chair *has* the same color as the table'. 'Of' and 'has', here, signal that we are speaking in terms of qualitative similarities and not real identity relations. But there appears to be no good reason for omitting terms such as 'color', or drawing this distinction between qualitative similarity and identity so sharply. 'A is the same color as *b*' has well-defined truth conditions, in spite of numerous attempts to claim that the applicable test should be whether '*a* is the same colored thing as *b*' has clear truth conditions.[12] After all, the same move might be made with any of the mass terms Geach is anxious to include in his framework: why '*a* is the same gold as *b*' and not '*a* is the same golden thing as *b*'? As Kraut observes, moreover, the relativity of identity can make sense only if distinctions between numerical and qualitative identity, in short, between particulars and properties, between identities and qualitative similarities, are also relative (79, 85,

---

12. See Dummett, pp. 85, 329–30, 562, 574; Kraut, pp. 79, 89–90.

90–91). There are therefore no good grounds on which to base the exclusion of cases of the sort Kraut has in mind.

I argue, then, that we should reject Geach's claim that '$a =_F b$' ought to entail 'Fa & Fb', on the grounds that the best argument for relative identity, namely, the argument from the possibility of revision, at best supports language relativism, not substantival relativism; thus the argument provides no support for the alleged entailment, for language relativism denies that it holds. Furthermore, even if substantival relativism can be defended, there are no grounds open to the substantival relativist for a distinction between cases that accord well with the implication and those which seem to be counterexamples to it.

The truth condition I have suggested, therefore, though it is accurate in the sense that it correctly represents Geach's intentions, is unsatisfactory on other grounds. I have tried to show that a consideration of the truth conditions that correspond to the views of Geach and Kraut indicates both that there is a very real distinction between relativity to a substantival and relativity to a discriminative framework, and that, of the two, relativity to a discriminative framework is to be preferred. How, then might we recast the truth condition in order to provide a reasonable account of relative identity relations, in the context of language relativism? I would like to suggest a criterion which is a minor revision of Kraut's:

'$a =_F b$' is true if and only if, for every F-predicate Q_F, $Q_F(a) \equiv Q_F(b)$.

where the Q_F's are, once again, those predicates which are relevant to the identification of F's; they constitute, in other words, the ideology of the theory in which '$=_F$' is an I-predicable.[13] This truth condition replaces Leibniz's law by guaranteeing that relative identity relations are equivalence relations and by providing that identicals are substitutable within those contexts in which the set of predicates relevant to identification remains unchanged. Thus the objection to Geach's position, and really to relative theories of identity in general, that relativity is incompatible with Leibniz's law, is

13. Compare, for example, Kraut, pp. 76–7. There is a slight difficulty here, for, as I have argued, the uniqueness of the theory concerned is questionable. The solution to this problem takes one far from the matters at hand, since different solutions, I am convinced, are appropriate to different predicates.

minimal in impact; the relative-identity theorist can reconstruct a logic of identity which is sufficient for most purposes
and for all purposes that he is willing to recognize as legitimate.

4. Reconstructing Classical Identity Theory

Before going further in the logic of identity, we must stop
to consider a dispute between classical and relative-identity
advocates which muddles our reconstruction. Many have
charged that if there is any semantic incompleteness to
sentences of the form '$a = b$', we should blame it not on the
incompleteness or meaninglessness of the identity relation,
but on a failure of reference. Thus, if '$(2, 3) = (4, 6)$' is
semantically incomplete, this is not because '$=$' is a pseudo-
relation, but because '$(2, 3)$' is ambiguous: are we referring to
the rational number or to the ordered pair? If we refer to rational numbers, the claim may be true, and, if to ordered
pairs, it is false. But in any case, we have a simple ambiguity
of reference, so the relativity of identity is not in question.[14]
We may put the same point in Dummett's language: between what are the relative identity relations supposed to
hold? The relative-identity theorist cannot answer, because
any answer would pick out some method of individuating
reality as privileged. All that can be said in response is "portions of the flux," "chunks of the amorphous lump," or "bits
of the passing show." Typically, however, we know between
what the identity relation is supposed to hold when we assert
'$a = b$'. If I say 'Cicero = Tully' and succeed in referring, I
mean to assert that they are the same person. Similarly, if I
assert '$(2, 3) = (4, 6)$' and make it clear that I am referring to
the construction of the rationals, the truth value of the claim
is determinate, and, if the context makes it clear that I am
referring to ordered pairs, the truth value is plainly falsehood. Only where the reference is ambiguous—and the
paradigm of this is 'this = that', a sentence involving
demonstratives—is there any indeterminacy in the semantics.

This issue has sparked a discussion of whether it is accept-

---

14. See Perry, pp. 185, 190; Stevenson, p. 157; Jack Nelson, "On the Alleged Incompleteness of Certain Identity Claims," *Canadian Journal of Philosophy*, III (1973): 105–13, p. 110n; Sydney Shoemaker, "Wiggins on Identity," *Philosophical Review*, LXXIX (1970): 529–544, p. 533; Dummett, pp.
545, 564, 571.

able to talk of "words", or whether this is sloppy speech to be replaced by talk of "type-words", "token-words", etc. It has also given rise to a discussion of the distinction between qualitative and numerical identity, and so between names and predicates, particulars and properties. But, as Kraut points out, these are the distinctions that the relative-identity theorist wants, if not to reject, at least to relativize. If we are speaking "colorese", for example, we may speak of 'red' as a name, for red is a particular from the perspective of that discriminative framework. Thus to say of my red car and my red hat that they are "the same" will not be to say that they share a quality, from the point of view of a language that does not distinguish objects having the same color, even though this is how we might translate it into our more usual talk of objects. Instead we can think of this as an assertion of a numerical identity between two bits of the passing show, both of which help to constitute the "scattered particular" red. Thus what we see as a particular, and what we take as a claim of numerical identity, depends upon the discriminative framework we mobilize at the time.

It may be objected that as soon as we refer in a fairly determinate way—to this *hat* and that *car*—the jig is up, and the distinction between qualitative and numerical identity reemerges. But the relative-identity theorist can claim that the distinction reappears only because the set of discriminative resources utilized in making the claim is revealed.

The moral Kraut draws—I think the correct moral—is that the distinction between these claims is specious. There is no difference between saying that identity is relative and saying that reference is frequently ambiguous; either way, the point is that there is a kind of incompleteness to claims such as '*a* = *b*' which must be filled, whether by specifying identification criteria or by clarifying the reference of the terms '*a*' and '*b*'. Whether the indeterminacy is ascribed to the terms or to the identity relation itself is a matter of taste; the sentence as a whole, however, requires an implicit or explicit specification of a discriminative framework for its truth value to be fully determinate. Thus the indeterminacy, we might say, is a function of the *sentence;* it may be localized in the terms of the assertion or in the identity relation, but that need not interest us philosophically. If in practice most identity statements have an unambiguous meaning, it is because the terms successfully refer, by virtue of supplying the context from which the relativization may be specified. We are thus left with a position which, though a significant revision of Geach's view, is nevertheless not very far from the spirit of the relative-identity thesis.

Granted, then, that there is a sort of relativization involved—whether the locus be the identity relation or the terms and their reference—should we embrace language relativism? I argue that we should not, because we can reconstruct a close approximation to classical identity theory, even making the concessions we might want to make to the advocate of relative identity. Consider the image of reality that Dummett conjures up, of an amorphous lump which may be carved up conceptually in a great variety of ways. Why can we not take the totality of these ways of individuating the flux and base an absolute conception of identity upon that? Dummett claims that the relative-identity theorist can respond only that the notion of the totality of conditions of individuation does not make sense, but Dummett sees little reason why it should not (566–7). In defense of the relative-identity advocate, however, Dummett's meaning is far from clear. How does a consideration of the totality of individuating or identifying conditions salvage absolute identity?

The beginnings of an answer may be found in Wittgenstein. Think of a claim of self-identity: '$a = a$', or in generalized form, '$(x)(x = x)$'. Though these are practically useless, says Wittgenstein, they nevertheless seem to reflect a paradigm: one can imagine an object, and see that it "fits" into itself.[15] The point, in our context, is that sentences such as '$(x)(x = x)$', 'Tully = Tully', 'Pegasus = Pegasus', etc., seem to be unexceptionable. My claim is that these sentences are quite unambiguously true, simply because there is no substantive, no discriminative framework, from the perspective of which an object might not be self-identical. We might think of absolute identity as a construction out of relative identity relations, accepting the quasi-Geachian conclusions of some of our previous arguments, but insisting that, roughly,

'$a = b$' is true if and only if, for any F, $a =_F b$.

This truth condition should make the classical identity theorist happy, since if we employ the analysis of the sentence '$a =_F b$' developed earlier, we obtain Leibniz's law.

15. Ludwig Wittgenstein, *Philosophical Investigations*, G. E. M. Anscombe, trans. (New York: Macmillan, 1958), p. 84.

But we should stress, in deference to the relative-identity theorist, that the notion of absolute identity that emerges here is derivative, defined in terms of relative identity relations: '$a =_F b$' is *not* analyzed into '$a = b$ & Fa & Fb'.

Our quantification over predicates or properties in the truth condition might disturb the Geachian, but this presents no insuperable problem. We can interpret the quantification substitutionally (a technique Geach himself employs in similar circumstances), and in any case, Geach's arguments that the quantification over predicates in Leibniz's law leads to semantic paradox are dubious. Furthermore, even on Geach's own terms, it is not clear that we must quantify over all predicates; Geach's position can be reformulated to speak of category terms, and we can get away with quantifying over only all category predicates, surely a more manageable collection than the set of all predicates. Finally, any problem involving this sort of metalinguistic quantification which afflicts my condition also afflicts Leibniz's law.

Still, there is a slight problem with the above formulation, since it makes the vast majority of identity claims we make about the world, without providing any specific frame of reference, false. This is the reason for my qualification "roughly" in the above; we can repair the situation by noting that the notion of semantic ambiguity is itself ambiguous. Geach's chief claim is that there is a sort of semantic ambiguity or indeterminacy about identity as it is usually construed. He argues that, unless a substantival term is supplied, the statement of identity is meaningless. Why? Why not false, or truth-value-less?

We might spell out three possibilities, as follows: the specification of a substantival might be

(1) a condition of *truth:* no identity statement can be true unless a substantival is understood or supplied. Thus we have that '$a = b$' implies '$a =_F b$' (for a specified substantival F).[16]

(2) a condition of *truth value:* no identity statement can be true or false unless a substantival is supplied. Thus we have that '$a = b$' presupposes '$a =_F b$' (for a specified substantival F).[17]

16. That this is for some *specified* substantival is critically important to the relative-identity thesis. For a look at what happens when 'specified' is omitted, see Leslie Stevenson, "Extensional and Intensional Logic for Criteria of Identity," *Logique et Analyse,* xx (1977): 268–285. The system collapses into classical identity theory.

17. The notion of presupposition is van Fraassen's. See his *Formal Semantics and Logic* (New York: Macmillan, 1971), pp. 154ff.

(3) a condition of *meaningfulness:* no identity statement can be meaningful unless a substantival is supplied.

Now (1) may be true, though uninteresting. Surely, if *a* and *b* are identical, there is some predicate *F* such that *a* is the same *F* as *b*. Option (3) is Geach's claim, though I have already attempted to argue that it is false; I have tried to reconstruct a meaning for the absolute identity relation, which makes clear that, even by the standards of the relative-identity theorist, absolute identity statements can be considered meaningful. To say that something is meaningless, after all, is a very strong claim: that the bit of language is not well formed, and, in particular, that no truth conditions at all are appropriate to it. Thus in giving truth conditions for absolute identity statements we have refuted Geach's claim. The same holds true of other forms of relativism, if we substitute 'language' or 'discriminative framework' for 'substantival' throughout the above.

The alternative I shall adopt, then, is (2), that certain identity statements are truth-valueless. My truth condition for absolute identity claims should then read:

$$'a = b' \text{ is true if, for all } F, a =_F b;$$
$$'a = b' \text{ is false if, for all } F, a \neq_F b;$$
$$'a = b' \text{ is truth-value-less otherwise.}$$

We thus please the classical identity theorist by reconstructing what is essentially Leibniz's law, though, in deference to the relative-identity theorist, we are left with truth-value gaps. Relativity to a discriminative framework thus riddles the theory of identity with holes of a special sort, without doing it any essential damage.

7 Pythagoreanism and Proxy Functions

In this chapter I shall consider Quine's claim that the specification of a proxy function is a necessary condition for ontological reduction. I shall argue that Quine's requirement has neither a philosophical nor a technical justification, since the account of reduction developed in chapter four has enough strength to withstand the assault of neo-Pythagoreanism. Finally I shall suggest that the solution to the problem of neo-Pythagoreanism, and of related "trivial" reductions, lies in epistemology.

1. *Neo-Pythagoreanism and the Löwenheim-Skolem Theorem*

Pythagoras, as is well known, believed that the world consisted of nothing but numbers. The modern neo-Pythagorean, being somewhat less audacious, believes that "one is entitled to countenance nothing more than positive integers in his ontology."[1] Now this would seem an absurd and unlikely doctrine, except for the Löwenheim-Skolem theorem, from which it gathers its force. Skolem develops two versions of the theorem:

Theorem 7.1. If a set of first-order formulas has a model in any nonempty domain, then it has a model in the domain of positive integers.

Theorem 7.2. If a set of first-order formulas has a model in a nonempty domain D, then it has a model in a countable subdomain of D, the terms occurring in the formulas retaining the same meaning in both models.[2]

Theorem 7.1 can be proved without the axiom of choice,

1. Gerald Massey, "Reflections on the Unity of Science," *Annals of the Japanese Association for the Philosophy of Science*, IV (1973); reprint, p. 11. All further parenthetical page references to Massey will be to this article, unless otherwise noted.

2. These are the versions presented by Massey, p. 12. See Thoralf Skolem, "Logico-combinatorial Investigations in the Satisfiability or Provability of Mathematical Propositions: A Simplified Proof of a Theorem by L. Löwenheim and Generalizations of the Theorem," in Jean van Heijenoort, ed., *From Frege to Gödel: A Sourcebook in Mathematical Logic, 1879–1931* (Cambridge, Mass.: Harvard, 1967): 254–263; also van Heijenoort, in van Heijenoort, ed., p. 253.

whereas Theorem 7.2 requires use of the axiom, and is thus a stronger thesis. By "retaining the same meaning in both models" I mean that the relations associated with the predicates in the set of formulas on the subdomain are restrictions of the relations on D to that subdomain.

The argument from the Löwenheim-Skolem theorem to neo-Pythagoreanism runs as follows: reduction essentially involves modeling, or preservation of structure. But we can model any theory in the natural numbers, by the Löwenheim-Skolem theorem. So any domain of objects can be reduced to the natural numbers. If we wish to focus on Theorem 7.2, rather than 7.1, we can claim that any theory commits us, at most, to a denumerable ontology; Theorem 7.2 shows that all but a countable number of entities may be dropped from the ontology of a theory without disturbing either truth values or meanings of assertions of the theory. But clearly we can reduce any denumerable ontology to a numerical one, simply by an enumeration function which we need in any case in order to demonstrate the countability of the ontology. Thus any theory can be reduced to a theory committing us to a Pythagorean ontology of numbers.

These arguments rely on a conception of reduction which is, in essence, model-theoretic; they depend on the possibility of constructing a model of any theory in the domain of the natural numbers. The account of reduction I have developed in chapter four, however, requires preservation of predicate structure, not merely preservation of truth value; thus, though there may be a model of any theory in the natural numbers, there is not a reduction in every case, for there are syntactic as well as semantic conditions to be fulfilled. The neo-Pythagorean thesis that we can dispense with any domain of objects in favor of the natural numbers, on my view, amounts to the claim that every theory can be reduced to one involving a commitment to nothing more than the natural numbers. That there is an arithmetical model is not enough; there must be a translation of each theory into arithmetic, or a similar theory, satisfying the conditions established in chapter four. And the Löwenheim-Skolem theorem does not provide any such translations.[3]

3. This is recognized by Quine, "Ontological Reduction and the World of Numbers," in *The Ways of Paradox and Other Essays* (Cambridge, Mass.: Harvard, 1976): 212–220, pp. 215–6; Leslie Tharp, "Ontological Reduction," *Journal of Philosophy*, LXVIII (1971): 151–164, p. 153; Michael Jubien, "Two Kinds of Reduction," *ibid.*, LXVI (1969): 533–541, pp. 539–40; Dale Gottlieb, "Ontological Reduction," *ibid.*, LXXIII (1976): 57–76, pp. 60–1. Further par-

Once we appreciate, however, that neo-Pythagoreanism must assert the reducibility of any theory to one committing us only to the natural numbers, we can recognize that the thesis is ambiguous. First, the quantificational structure of the principle is not quite clear. We can envision at least two plausible readings:

(p1) For any theory T, there is another theory T' to which T is reducible and which commits us to nothing but the positive integers.

(p2) There is a theory T' that commits us to nothing but the positive integers, to which any theory T can be reduced.

If we were to state the thesis as the claim that any theory may be reduced to arithmetic, we would beg the question in favor of reading (p2), by assuming that there is one theory of the natural numbers, viz. arithmetic, to which any theory must be reducible. Clearly (p2) implies (p1), so I shall begin by examining (p2), as the stronger neo-Pythagorean assertion. The thesis on this reading suggests that there is a single theory committing us to the natural numbers, to which any theory at all can be reduced. But this brings us to a second ambiguity in the thesis: what theory of the natural numbers should play this role? Since virtually nobody has ever advocated neo-Pythagoreanism, we cannot answer by pointing to the claims of neo-Pythagoreans. But it seems only fair to allow a hypothetical advocate the power of full number theory. To restrict the thesis to one concerning Presburger arithmetic, or Robinson arithmetic, or some other restricted system, is to limit the neo-Pythagorean unnecessarily, so long as we are willing to accept stronger theories of the numbers. I shall thus interpret (p2) as contending, in effect, that every theory we accept can be reduced to elementary number theory. For all practical purposes, this may be regarded as the system presented by S. C. Kleene.[4]

Quine has made the most significant, and perhaps the only attempt to formulate an account of reduction that avoids neo-Pythagoreanism. Since he does not sharply distinguish (p1) and (p2), it is not clear in which form the thesis motivates his concern. But in any case, Quine proposes an additional criterion for ontological reduction to stymie the arguments in favor of an ontology of numbers:

---

enthetical page references to Quine in this chapter will be to "Ontological Reduction and the World of Numbers," unless noted otherwise.

4. *Introduction to Metamathematics* (Groningen: Wolters-Noordhoff, 1971), pp. 181–216.

This third condition is that we be able to specify what I shall call a *proxy function*: a function which assigns one of the new things, in this example a pure number, to each of the old things—each of the impure numbers of temperature (217).

Say that we are concerned with the reduction of one theory, T, to another, T'. Let 'Dom(T)' and 'Dom(T')' represent the universes of discourse of T and T', respectively, and let g be a function from the n-place predicates of T, for each n, into open sentences of T' in n free variables. Then a proxy function f is a mapping from Dom(T) into Dom(T') such that '$F(x_1, \ldots, x_n)$' holds just in case '$g(F) (f(x_1), \ldots, f(x_n))$' does also (218). Quine adds this requirement to an account of reduction very similar to that developed in chapter four. But the addition of the proxy-function condition alters substantially this concept of reduction. Without the demand for such a function, reduction is essentially a linguistic matter, which we can explicate by considering a theory as a set of first-order sentences, in a highly abstract way. Reduction, on my account, is based upon the eliminability of reference to objects of certain kinds. On Quine's paradigm, however, extralinguistic considerations invade the concept of reduction, for a proxy function relates objects, not linguistic items. Quine is forced to treat theories as sets of first-order sentences together with interpretations and universes consisting of determinate sets of objects. The problem of whether or not we should demand a proxy function's specification as a condition of the adequacy of an ontological reduction amounts to the problem of whether ontological reduction is a solely linguistic matter.

Quine's introduction of the proxy-function requirement is ad hoc: there are no independent philosophical motivations for making the demand.[5] As Charles Chihara indicates, "it is as if some board game had been ruined by the discovery of a simple procedure which enabled the beginning side to always win and the problem was to figure out a way of saving the game by changing the rules slightly" (126). Quine virtually admits as much. His argument for the requirement is that "we have in fact narrowed it to where, as it seems to me, the

---

5. See Charles Chihara, *Ontology and the Vicious Circle Principle* (Ithaca, N.Y.: Cornell, 1973), pp. 126, 134; Tharp, p. 156; Massey, p. 16; Richard Grandy, "On What There Need Not Be," *Journal of Philosophy*, LXVI (1969): 809–811, p. 809.

things we should like to count as reduction do so count and the rest do not" (218).

The charge that Quine's requirement is ad hoc does not refute his position, but insists that it is incomplete, in the sense that some independent justification for the demand for the specification of proxy functions is required. But the strategy underlying the use of reduction is Wittgensteinian: we show that the troublesome commitments of some discourse are not really problematic by showing that the discourse itself is avoidable. The theory to be reduced, then, can be eliminated in favor of another theory that allows us to do the same job in our conceptual scheme. But if this is what reduction is all about, then what kind of justification *could* we have for demanding the specification of proxy functions? If reduction essentially involves showing that certain linguistic usages are avoidable, then why should reduction involve any relation between extralinguistic items which cannot be expressed in purely linguistic terms? If reduction is viewed as elimination, then, there are no good reasons for thinking that proxy functions have any significance with regard to the adequacy of reductions. Quine's requirement therefore contradicts a theory of reduction as elimination; surprisingly, this is a theory to which Quine apparently adheres.[6]

We cannot, therefore, justify Quine's demand for the specification of a proxy function as a necessary condition for the adequacy of an ontological reduction from a philosophical point of view. Surprisingly, Quine's requirement has no technical justification either. It *is* a technical success: the demand for specifying a proxy function does preclude a reduction of every domain to that of the natural numbers alone. The Löwenheim-Skolem theorem does not enable us to specify such a function in general; in theories in which identity is primitive or definable, the proxy-function requirement rules out any reduction in the cardinality of a domain, so, in some cases, apparently, no proxy function even exists.[7] Thus we can show that there are theories that are not reducible to a theory of the positive integers, on Quine's account; any theory with an uncountable domain appears to resist such a reduction. Quine's proxy-function requirement, therefore, is

6. See, for example, *Word and Object* (Cambridge, Mass.: MIT Press, 1960), pp. 260–1.

7. See Chihara, pp. 123–125; Tharp, p. 155; Jubien, p. 533. Compare Quine, "Ontological Reduction and the World of Numbers," pp. 218–9.

a success in blocking the objectionable consequences of the Löwenheim-Skolem theorem, even, perhaps, if it is weakened to require only the existence, rather than the specification of a proxy function. Nevertheless, the linguistic approach to reduction taken in chapter four already blocks neo-Pythagoreanism. We can demonstrate that certain important theories cannot be reduced to arithmetic, even in the sense of full elementary number theory. We can show, using the results of Solomon Feferman and Jan Mycielski, that, for any theories T and T', if a suitable version of the arithmetized consistency statement for T can be proved in T', then T' is not interpretable in T.[8] But we can show that some such version of a consistency statement for number theory is provable in set theory (for example, in ZF); it follows that set theory cannot be reduced to arithmetic. Thus various strengthenings of ZF, with the addition of the continuum hypothesis, or axioms of the existence of an inaccessible or measurable cardinal, also fail to reduce to arithmetic. To mention a final example, if we add to number theory the arithmetized consistency statement for number theory, the resulting theory cannot be interpreted in number theory alone.[9] In general, any theory in which the concept of arithmetical truth can be expressed fails to reduce to arithmetic, by Tarski's theorem. As a result, the view of reduction as linguistic elimination does not have the consequence that all theories reduce to arithmetic; not even all mathematical theories reduce to arithmetic. Thus, the linguistic account of reduction does not fall prey to the general trivialization of ontology threatened by the Löwenheim-Skolem theorem. If we read the neo-Pythagorean thesis as (p2), then, it can be ruled out of court on technical grounds alone, even without the proxy-function requirement.

If neo-Pythagoreanism is to have a serious hearing, therefore, it will have to be in the form (p1). Does the thesis in its weaker form have any plausibility? We can in turn divide this question into two: does (p1) have any reasonable claim to being true? and does (p1), if true, demonstrate that we need be committed to nothing other than the positive integers in

8. See Feferman, "Arithmetization of Metamathematics in a General Setting," *Fundamenta Mathematicae*, xlix (1960): 35–92, theorems 6.2 and 6.5; Mycielski, "A Lattice of Interpretability Types of Theories," *Journal of Symbolic Logic*, xlii (1977): 297–305, p. 303.

9. See Feferman, theorem 6.5; and theorem 4.9 of chapter four above.

our ontology? As we shall see, the answers to these questions are 'yes' and 'no', respectively.

I shall begin by noting two points. First, ontological commitment may be understood as pertaining to theories or to persons. These notions are very closely related; which depends on which is a question best left for another time. But ultimately we care about the commitments of persons, not theories, in ontology, since we are concerned with what *we* are committed to in our general account of the world. It may be that the best way to find out what commitments we have is to examine the structure of our theories; it is crucial, however, that we examine not just any arbitrary theories that come down the pike but those which we grant acceptance. Imagine a very elaborate theory of ghosts, witches, warlocks, spirits, and other Halloweenish entities. Though this theory may have very onerous ontological commitments to a wide variety of unsavory objects, we need not care about its commitments in dealing with matters of ontology, because we do not believe the theory to be true. Thus, in determining what *our* ontological commitments are, we need consider only those theories which we accept. Second, we generally think that we have a fairly clear impression, however it may be derived, of the natural numbers. A number of theories may be appropriate and correct theories of the numbers — Presburger arithmetic, Robinson arithmetic, Peano arithmetic, etc. — but these tend to be distinguished on the basis of the strength of their vocabularies and their axioms. Presburger and Robinson arithmetics, for example, are different portions of full first-order number theory. Strength of vocabulary does make an important metatheoretical difference: arithmetic with only addition may be decidable, whereas arithmetic with both addition and multiplication cannot be. Nevertheless, these theories are closely related, in the sense that they do not disagree in those areas where they share the same vocabulary.

When we say, therefore, that, given any theory T, there is a theory T' to which T reduces and which commits us only to the positive integers, we must be careful about what sort of commitment is involved. Though T' may be committed to nothing but the natural numbers, we care about its commitments only if we think it worthy of acceptance. Consequently, *we* need be committed only to the natural numbers just in case every theory we accept reduces to some other theory we accept which forces only those commitments. Thus, for (p1) to demonstrate the neo-Pythagorean thesis, the theories of the natural numbers (the "T's") must be worthy of acceptance as legitimate and correct theories of the numbers. Consequently, though these theories may differ, in matters of similarity type, decidability, etc., they must not disagree. If the theories did not concur, their union would not be consistent, and in that case it would make no sense to say that we accept all of them. Furthermore, the theories must not commit us to controversial or questionable theses about the numbers; we must accept the theories in their entirety as descriptions of the positive integers.

I have already given examples of theories that would be acceptable candidates for different T's in this account. But these theories tend to be related as parts to a whole, as theories with limited vocabularies to supertheories with stronger expressive powers. Thus, it might be acceptable to have some theories reduce to Presburger arithmetic, whereas others reduce only to elementary number theory. But if this is what we have in mind as a parsing of (p1), it differs only trivially from (p2). Any theory that reduces to Presburger arithmetic or Robinson arithmetic *a fortiori* reduces to full number theory. Thus, on this interpretation, (p1) is equivalent to (p2): if (p1) holds, and the T's are related in the way described, then there is a unique theory to which any other theory reduces and which commits us only to positive integers. As we have already seen, however, (p2) is false; there is no such theory. If (p1) is to be taken seriously, therefore, we must find another interpretation of the weak neo-Pythagorean position.

2. Axiomatic Theories

Before searching for another interpretation of (p1), we would be wise to review some technical results concerning interpretability relations. We have already seen that there are theorems concerning the noninterpretability of certain theories:

Theorem 4.9. For any supertheory T of Peano arithmetic, $T \cup \{\text{Con } T\}$ is not interpretable in T.

Theorem 7.3. For any theories T and T', if $T' \vdash \text{Con } T$, then $T' \nleq T$.

But there are also theorems suggesting that a large number of theories can be interpreted in arithmetic, or closely related theories. Thus we find:

Theorem 7.4. For any satisfiable first-order formula A,

there is an effective method for finding open sentences of elementary number theory which, when substituted for the predicate letters in A, make A true.[10]

Theorem 7.5 Any consistent and decidable theory is interpretable in elementary number theory (Peano arithmetic).[11]

Theorem 4.8. For any theories S and T, if Peano arithmetic is a subtheory of S and T has an arithmetically definable set of axioms, then $T \leqslant S \cup \{\text{Con } T\}$.

The first two of these theorems (4.9 and 7.3) indicate that some theories are not interpretable in arithmetic. But, if so, how can we characterize which theories *can* be interpreted in number theory? The answer, at least in part, is provided by the next three theorems. Though the proof of the Löwenheim-Skolem theorem takes the predicates of any first-order theory and reinterprets them as predicates of numbers, we cannot show, in general, that these predicates are definable in arithmetic. Nevertheless, under certain conditions the predicates can be expressed in arithmetical terms.

The theorems, however, point out that 'expressed in arithmetical terms' is ambiguous. Quine, for example, asserts that the predicates of a theory are expressible in arithmetical terms if the theory is completely axiomatizable (216–7). We may interpret this in two ways. Quine may mean 'completely axiomatizable' as 'complete *and* axiomatizable'; if so, since complete and axiomatizable theories are decidable (assuming that they are consistent), this follows from Theorem 7.5. In contrast, Quine may be speaking less formally, intending 'completely axiomatizable' to mean 'as a whole, axiomatizable', which of course amounts simply to 'axiomatizable'. Axiomatizable theories have arithmetically definable sets of axioms, of course, so this follows from Theorem 4.8. But theories that have arithmetically definable sets of axioms without being decidable reduce to arithmetic in a sense quite different from that in which decidable theories so reduce. The arithmetically definable yet undecidable theory can be reduced only to a slight enlargement of arithmetic, consisting of elementary number theory supplemented by the arithmetized consistency statement for the theory in question. Decidable theories do not require that arithmetic be

10. See David Hilbert and Paul Bernays, *Grundlagen der Mathematik* II (Berlin: Springer-Verlag, 1968), p. 253; Quine, "Implicit Definition Sustained," in *The Ways of Paradox and Other Essays*: 133–136, pp. 133–4.

11. This is in fact a corollary of Theorem 4.8. The proof of decidability and thus of consistency (in nontrivial cases) of decidable theories can be carried out in arithmetic.

supplemented in this way; for in actual cases the proof of decidability, and thus, in nontrivial cases, of consistency may be carried out in arithmetic. Let us say that decidable theories can be interpreted in arithmetic, *simpliciter*; undecidable but arithmetically definable theories will be said to be interpretable in an *amplified* arithmetic, i.e., arithmetic together with the relevant consistency statement.

Strictly speaking, then, (p1) is false. But we cannot dismiss neo-Pythagoreanism so neatly, for, within a fairly broad range, first-order theories do turn out to reduce to elementary number theory. If we read the neo-Pythagorean thesis as (p2), then the thesis is true within the limited realm of decidable theories. This, perhaps, need not trouble us greatly; few significant theories are decidable. Any theory in which arithmetic can be interpreted, even in a very weak form, for example, is undecidable. Thus we might view decidability as a kind of limiting result, since any theory with the resources to represent addition and multiplication at the same time will turn out to have, as it were, too much expressive power to be decidable.

But the neo-Pythagorean thesis, understood as (p1), presents a more substantial puzzle. Though (p1) is false when we speak of *all* theories, it is true when we limit our concern to theories with arithmetically definable sets of axioms. Two lines of thought might lead us to think that this is a disturbing result. First, many of the theories we in fact accept and use are axiomatic in structure. These will turn out to reduce to an amplified arithmetic, given the linguistic account of reduction of chapter four. Second, we might think, as Leslie Tharp insists (161), that any theory accepted at any given time has an effectively specifiable (i.e., recursive) set of axioms; can we even advocate the truth of sentences not so specifiable? If the answer is no, then any theory we advocate at any given time can be reduced to an amplified arithmetic. In allowing for a variety of theories of the numbers to which our everyday theories reduce, therefore, (p1) may seem to show that any theory we are likely to care about reduces to one committing us to nothing but a Pythagorean ontology of numbers.

Consider Tharp's challenge first. Though we operate in mathematics with axiomatic theories at many crucial junctures, we can show that these theories do not exhaust the truths of the language at hand. Von Neumann-Gödel-Bernays set theory, for example, has a finite number of axioms, but we can show that these axioms and their consequences do not exhaust the truths of set theory. Only in a very extended sense, then, could we say that set theory has been reduced to elementary number theory or some extension thereof.

Nonetheless, quite a few theories with arithmetically definable sets of axioms will so reduce; should this result upset us? Other admittedly counterintuitive results follow from a linguistic account of reduction. Any theory, it turns out, can be interpreted in an inconsistent theory, since as long as we have some translation of the theory at hand into the language of the inconsistent theory, the theorems of the original theory go into theorems under the translation; every statement is a theorem of an inconsistent theory. This is analogous to the fact that any argument with inconsistent premises is valid. Though this result, too, is counterintuitive, it does not disrupt the general theory. Are the results concerning the reduction of any axiomatizable theory to number theory, in an amplified form, troublesome in a more serious way?

Theorem 4.8 shows that any axiomatizable theory may be interpreted in number theory supplemented by an additional axiom asserting the consistency of the relevant theory. But the theories of the numbers we obtain as a result of this operation do not constitute number theory in the usual sense of the term. They are in general much stronger theories, and, if the theory to be reduced is at all complex or controversial, we may have substantial doubts about the truth of the consistency statement for the theory. Any theory so simple that its consistency is not controversial probably can be interpreted in arithmetic already. Furthermore, we are asked to adopt no new theory of the integers, but a collection of "arithmetics", or, at least, a different "arithmetic" for each theory we contemplate reducing. At best, then, Theorem 4.8 supports neo-Pythagoreanism in its weaker version (p1), but so interpreted that the various theories of the numbers have no close relation to one another. It is tempting to say, then, that these theories are not really arithmetics at all, for the theses they assert above our ordinary arithmetical theorems are likely to be somewhat controversial, and will surely differ significantly in character from our more typically arithmetical theses.

The neo-Pythagorean, however, may not be convinced. For we are committed to the *truth* of the theories we accept, and thus to the truth of those theories we accept which we wish to reduce by way of the Löwenheim-Skolem theorem or one of its variants. The commitment to the consistency of these theories, therefore, appears to be far less onerous than the commitment to truth which we are already willing to bear. Moreover, the amplified arithmetics that contain these at most mildly controversial theses certainly commit us to nothing other than the natural numbers. So we appear to face a dilemma. Even if we are willing to accept the reductions of decidable theories to arithmetic, on the grounds that decidable theories are not very interesting or conceptually powerful, we would like to deny that any arithmetically definable theory reduces, in an ontologically interesting sense, to a theory committing us only to positive integers. But we can deny this only if we alter the linguistic account of reduction, and any such alteration will tend to be ad hoc, without any philosophical justification. Since our entire analysis of reduction roots the notion in the eliminability of linguistic forms, such an independent justification does not seem to be forthcoming. So we must either reconcile ourselves to the reduction of arithmetically definable theories, or, like Quine, appeal to an ad hoc and ultimately nonlinguistic solution.

If we are to avoid ad hoc restrictions, and maintain a theory of reduction founded upon linguistic eliminability, we must embrace the reductions of decidable and arithmetically definable theories as legitimate. But this does not ruin our linguistic account of ontological reduction. Recall that any argument with inconsistent premises is valid. Why does this not damage the propositional calculus? We will not accept any such argument as *sound*, and soundness is what we care about in applications. We know that we cannot properly be in a position to assert jointly the premises of the argument; the argument's validity, then, though it is counterintuitive, is not troublesome. The argument violates other norms that characterize the arguments that hold interest for us. Similarly, when a theory reduces to an inconsistent theory on the linguistic paradigm, no theoretical shock waves are produced; we can never truly assert the inconsistent theory. In this case too, there are norms that characterize the class of theories we care about as possible reducing theories, and these norms exclude inconsistent theories.

I shall argue that similar norms rule out some of the reductions sanctioned by Theorems 4.8 and 7.5. Though they satisfy the formal criteria of reduction, certain norms rule them out as uninteresting cases of the general formula, just as arguments with inconsistent premises are ruled out as uninteresting, though formally valid. We must distinguish, then, the formal from the nonformal criteria for reduction, just as we distinguish validity from soundness when speaking of arguments. Dale Gottlieb has thus distinguished the *legitimacy* from the *desirability* of a reduction.[12] Some of the reductions that arise from the Löwenheim-Skolem theorem and its variants we shall classify as legitimate though undesirable, in the sense that they satisfy the formal, but not the nonformal conditions for the adequacy of a reduction.

What are these norms, the nonformal criteria that can separate reductions having ontological significance from those having only formal interest? To answer this question, we must ask why neo-Pythagoreanism seems so upsetting in the first place. If all questions of ontology and commitment distill down to commitments to positive integers then, according to Quine, ontology becomes a trivial matter (216). Gerald Massey similarly exclaims that, if the neo-Pythagorean thesis is true, it "constitutes a scandal no less serious than Hume's scandal of induction" (17). Indeed, the avoidance of neo-Pythagoreanism is often regarded as a criterion of accounts of ontological reduction. But why? What is so repulsive about neo-Pythagoreanism? Quine may think that it ruins the fun of ontology, but, from the perspective of the neo-Pythagorean, it gives us a determinate answer to oft-disputed questions concerning what exists: "0, 1, 2, . . . and nothing else". Yet it tends to be disturbing that rocks, trees, and even electrons and persons are really logical constructions out of natural numbers. As Massey observes, "when you and I and the familiar things of daily experience are the candidates for elimination, there is cause for uneasiness if not alarm. Creeping computerization threatens to reduce us to numbers, figuratively speaking. Neo-Pythagoreanism purports to effect that reduction literally" (12–3). It may be shocking to imagine yourself as a cloud of subatomic particles; how much worse to imagine yourself as nothing but a logical complex of natural numbers! As philosophers, of course, we are obliged to analyze our repulsion for these consequences. I suspect that we rebel against neo-Pythagoreanism for essentially epistemological reasons. The norms we invoke to preclude neo-Pythagorean reductions from having ontological significance, therefore, have to be epistemological in character.

To specify these norms, we must distinguish what *can* be reduced to what from what *ought to* be reduced to what. This distinction, though hardly new, is often overlooked, and in-

12. Gottlieb, p. 75. Further parenthetical page references to Gottlieb will be to "Ontological Reduction," unless noted otherwise.

deed is obscured by talk of reducibility or conditions for reduction. 'T is reducible to T''' may mean that T can be reduced to T', or that T should be reduced to T'. Of course, to
say that T ought to be reduced to T' is to say that the reduction of T to T' meets the nonformal as well as the formal
conditions for reduction. Thus, where ontological reduction
is concerned, it is not controversial that 'ought' implies 'can'.

To illustrate this distinction, imagine a very simple geographical theory, with one two-place predicate F, interpreted
as 'has a larger area than', and ranging over nations. The
axioms of this theory might be:

(1) $(x) -Fxx$

(2) $(x)\ (y)\ (Fxy \supset -Fyx)$

(3) $(x)\ (y)\ (z)\ (Fxy\ \&\ Fyz \supset Fxz)$

Now, by theorem 7.5, this theory has an arithmetical translation. In fact, to obtain an interpretation that will do the trick,
we need only interpret 'F' as '$>$'. Theorems clearly go into
theorems, and we thus have a formally acceptable reduction.
That there is more than this to be considered, G. D. W. Berry
points out:

> But would the mere existence of this interpretation
> tempt the geographer, or any of us, to prefer it to the
> original one? Would the fact that the original theory can
> be arithmetically interpreted lead anyone to claim that it
> *should be*, and the land-masses and peoples pre-
> supposed by the initial interpretation can justifiably be
> rejected and the whole earth considered, Pythagoras-
> wise, as a congeries of numbers?[13]

What can be reduced to what?, I suggest, is a question to
which we can give a formally precise answer. Chapter four
has attempted to provide that answer. But the question, What
ought to be reduced to what?, is far broader and more
difficult to analyze. It is, in a broad sense, an epistemological
question.

Berry asserts that our "wide background of belief" determines which interpretations ought to be taken seriously.

13. "On the Ontological Significance of the Löwenheim-Skolem
Theorem," in *Academic Freedom, Logic and Religion* (Philadelphia: University of Pennsylvania Press, 1953): 39–55, p. 53. Emphasis in original.

Charles Chihara stresses the significance of ties with sense experience, and Gottlieb, more generally, considers the "epistemic structure" and "cognitive role" of a theory to provide an answer. All three agree with Leslie Tharp that "epistemological considerations are the source, and a valid source, of one's discomfort" concerning neo-Pythagoreanism.[14] In our geographical example, why do we feel reluctant to dispense with nations in favor of numbers? Surely it is because we come to geographical knowledge in a way dramatically different from that we use to achieve arithmetical knowledge. Our axioms have little empirical import, but a fuller theory might contain sentences such as 'The Soviet Union is larger than Ecuador', which we might translate, say, as '8603000 > 104506'. The epistemic differences between these assertions are immense. We could hardly conduct our everyday affairs by using numerical reductions of this sort, even though eliminability in this sense is what reduction is all about.

Interestingly, Quine's proxy-function requirement cannot aid us by ridding us of these troublesome reductions. The reduction of the geographical theory to arithmetic goes through even when we employ Quine's more stringent standard of reduction. Specifying a proxy function is not very difficult: 'has an area of . . . square miles' provides precisely the required relation. Thus the epistemologically puzzling reductions cannot be eliminated from the picture by Quine's appeal to a proxy-function requirement; his analysis may get rid of some objectionable reductions, but others survive.

A stipulation that is more to the point is that of Ernest Nagel, who recognizes the significance of epistemology in the fulfillment of the condition of connectability. Nagel demands that there be some empirically confirmable link between the vocabularies of the theories involved in a reduction. Thus, in the case of empirical theories, the degree of empirical support for connecting assumptions may serve as a nonformal condition of reduction helping us to recognize those reductions which are interesting from an ontological point of view. Such a condition is not available generally, however; specifically, it fails in mathematics and in other theories ostensibly committing us to abstract entities.

Indeed, it is fairly safe to assume that no formal, extensional criterion of ontological reduction can eliminate alleged reductions that are epistemological travesties. But how can

14. See Berry, p. 54; Chihara, pp. 126–7; Gottlieb, p. 66; Tharp, p. 162.

we amend the account to handle such cases? How can we incorporate epistemology in our over-all theory of ontological reduction?

3. Reduction and Epistemology

Perhaps the most obvious reason for being suspicious of arithmetical Löwenheim-Skolem reductions is that the translation of a theory concerning some finite realm of objects other than numbers into arithmetic makes it impossible to see how we might acquire any new knowledge. If we translate a geographical theory into a theory of numbers, how do we find out new facts about geographical entities? We must think of things in geographical terms, not in number-theoretic terms, if we are ever to advance beyond an abecedarian stage. To see whether Vietnam is larger than Cambodia, or vice versa, we have to do some empirical investigation; no amount of poring over textbooks and theorems of number theory will help us to find the answer. It seems, then, that the geographical theory cannot be eliminated after all. We may rid ourselves of the old vocabulary so long as we are not interested in saying anything new or interesting about the original objects, but when we want to discover something, or say something novel, we must work with the original objects rather than with their images under the translation. An even stronger point may be made concerning the amplified arithmetics to which any arithmetically definable theory reduces. Given a theory T, we have reason to assert Con T, the arithmetized consistency statement for T, only by virtue of thinking about the actual content of T, i.e., T's "real" subject matter, not by virtue of thinking about numbers. Formally, for example, Zermelo-Fraenkel set theory can be reduced to elementary number theory supplemented by the arithmetized consistency statement for ZF. But for this to have any ontological significance, the reduction must allow us to cut down our ontological commitments. And we have no independent reason for thinking that this particular version of amplified arithmetic is true. The only reason we have for taking Con ZF to be true would have to come from reflection on the content of ZF, i.e., on set theory. It turns out, therefore, that, in general, amplified arithmetics have no epistemological foundation except that which they derive from the relevant nonarithmetical theories. Reductions to amplified arithmetics thus take us from theories, our knowledge of which we may be able to explain, to theories, the epistemic status of which is highly unclear and derivative.[15] These examples stray far from the usual case of reduction, where reduction amounts to an epistemological advance. When we reduce real numbers to sequences of rationals, for example, we cast light on the nature of the theories concerned; for one who relied on intuition, geometrical analogy, etc., in dealing with the reals, the reduction offers an increase in precision that actually assists research and the acquisition of knowledge. Similarly, the reduction of temperature to mean kinetic energy of molecules furthers the process of inquiry, by suggesting new parameters, new hypotheses, new principles of organization, etc. Thus many reductions aid our understanding of the phenomena under study. Reductions employing Theorems 4.8 and 7.5, however, among others, may obscure our understanding. They do not typify reductions, as far as epistemology is concerned; indeed they are unusual in the sense that they are often epistemologically unhelpful, if not disastrous.

We might demand fulfillment of another condition for the success of ontological reduction, therefore, which would require that a reduction be epistemically enlightening. Thus far, however, our account of reduction has been linguistic in character; is this extra criterion linguistic or nonlinguistic? I shall argue that any condition taking into account the epistemic impact of reduction must be extralinguistic. To see why this is so, I shall examine Dale Gottlieb's attempt to incorporate an epistemological criterion within a linguistic framework.

Gottlieb's first attempt at a criterion is (C1): "An ontological reduction of T to T' must preserve the epistemic structure of the language of our most comprehensive theory" (67). For Gottlieb, epistemic structure is the most important aspect of a theory's "cognitive role." Gottlieb allows the notion of a cognitive role to remain ambiguous. But the epistemic structure of a theory is the totality of the relations of rational support that hold among the sentences of the theory (67). Relations of implication, confirmation, explanation, "analytic" entailment, etc., are thus included in the notion of epistemic structure. And "in general, any relation R among sentences

15. The point concerning the acquisition of knowledge has been noticed before, by, for example, Gottlieb, p. 63; also Tharp, pp. 161–2. For the extension of the point to amplified arithmetics, I owe thanks to Charles Parsons.

will contribute to epistemic structure if a belief in S may be at least partially defended by citing a justified belief in S' and the fact that $S'RS$" (67).

The requirement that epistemic structure be preserved, however, fails as a criterion for ontological reduction. As Gottlieb himself points out, any translation at all alters the deductive relations between sentences, thus altering epistemic structure (68). Of course, this occurs only across the boundaries of theories, not necessarily within them. Thus, after the reduction of thermodynamics to statistical mechanics, we might attempt to justify a belief about temperatures by appealing to facts about kinetic energy; before the reduction, such an appeal was not possible. We need to distinguish, then, the epistemic structure of a theory from the epistemic structure of knowledge as a whole. The reduction of T to T' need not change the epistemic structure of T or of T', but does change the epistemic structure of the larger theory, $T \cup T'$, and so of the entire body of our knowledge. Furthermore, the utility of a reduction frequently depends upon these alterations in epistemic structure: the reduction of thermodynamics to statistical mechanics is important precisely because it does make available new relations of confirmation, support, etc. To prevent us from changing the epistemic structure of our most comprehensive theory is thus to prevent us from making any epistemic advance by way of reduction.

Recognizing the inadequacy of (C1), Gottlieb suggests (C2): "An ontological reduction of T to T' must preserve the essential features of the epistemic roles of the sentences of T" (69). (C2) weakens (C1) by distinguishing essential from nonessential features of the epistemic role of a sentence or theory; that distinction, therefore, is crucial to the success of (C2) as a criterion for ontological reduction. Gottlieb fails, nevertheless, to provide any account of the distinction, though he attempts to clarify it with examples. That arithmetical sentences are not open to refutation by simple observation, he argues, is essential to the epistemic structure of arithmetic (69). Similarly, microreductions figure as essential features of epistemic structure; Gottlieb argues that no numerical ontology can be adequate, because microreduction relations will disappear under the numerical translation (75). This, of course, assumes some antecedent notion of reduction—indeed, of ontological reduction—which does not appear to be available.

Whatever the precise lines of the distinction might be,

Gottlieb claims that the fulfillment of (C2) suffices to show the epistemic equivalence of two theories (76). On the view of reduction as elimination, however, reducibility relations are interpretability relations, where interpretability is a reflexive and transitive ordering relation. It is not an equivalence relation, for it is not symmetrical. Gottlieb's (C2), insofar as it suffices to demonstrate epistemic equivalence, does satisfy symmetry. Indeed, Gottlieb draws inspiration from the fact that some otherwise adequate reductions introduce alien implications by way of the translation from one theory into another. A theory about numbers, for example, might be translated into sentences that entail sentences about unicorns. Such a reduction, Gottlieb says, is inherently illegitimate (65-6).

When are such alien implications acceptable, and when are they not? If they pertain to the essential features of the epistemic role or structure of a theory, then it seems that according to Gottlieb they must be unacceptable; if not, there is no reason why they should not be welcomed. The distinction between essential and inessential features, as I have pointed out, is not very clear. Moreover, our analysis of ontological reduction allows alien implications, even within the reducing theory. An interpretation of the language of T into the language of T' interprets T into T' just in case, for any formula A of the language of T, the translation of A under the interpretation is a theorem of T' if A is a theorem of T. This definition is conditional rather than biconditional in form because we want to allow that the reducing theory may *add* to our knowledge of the objects of the reduced theory. Hence the body of sentences we are willing to assert about T-objects may grow once we assimilate them to T'-objects. Thus, the reduction of thermodynamics to statistical mechanics may give us more knowledge about temperature than we had before, even, perhaps, adding some knowledge we can express strictly in the language of thermodynamics alone. This is the reason I rejected strong interpretability as an account of reduction in chapter four. Gottlieb's criterion has much the same effect; it guarantees a sort of symmetry in the relations between theories involved in a reduction. Strong interpretability focuses on alien implications that might be introduced within the reduced theory; (C2) considers implications outside that theory as well.

In any event, (C2) appears to cut much too broadly. Alien implications are not in themselves objectionable; they lead us to label certain reductions as counterintuitive, but they also enable other reductions to contribute to the acquisition of knowledge. When we reduce thermodynamics, Gottlieb says, we do not alter the essential features of the epistemic role of the theory in our discourse as a whole. Nor do we run afoul of microreduction relations. But this reduction certainly alters our conception of thermodynamics in relation to the over-all structure of our knowledge and also changes our understanding of what microreduces to what. There is no change, in other words, only if we imagine ourselves *already* conceiving of temperature as a function of kinetic energy of microparticles. What we take as essential, and what we take as inessential, depends upon the role we assign a theory in the context of our discourse as a whole. Recall that Gottlieb's discussion of microreducibility relations presupposes some prior notion of reduction, which is not available; we can hardly use the concept of reduction to formulate an added criterion for reduction. Gottlieb's inclusion of microreducibility relations in the set of essential features of epistemic structure thus demonstrates the reliance of that notion on reduction, rather than the other way around. Relations between temperature and kinetic energy remain constant within our epistemic structure only if we have already imagined such a relation, but the reduction itself has altered our conception of what temperature and energy are.

In short, the epistemic role of our theories in the structure of our knowledge depends upon their interpretability relations and, more particularly, upon their reducibility relations. What we take as essential to epistemic structure therefore depends on what theories we take as fundamental and which others we reduce to them. The features we take as essential, then, are more a function of reductive relations than an arbiter of them. What we take as essential to epistemic structure does not determine which reductions we sanction as properly ontological; it is more nearly correct to say that which reductions we sanction as ontological determines what we take as essential. At the very least, there is a symbiotic relationship between the two. Any additional criterion for ontological reduction must be sought elsewhere.

Finally, Gottlieb's approach confuses the distinction between the issues What can be reduced to what? and What ought to be reduced to what? Consider the case of two theories that reduce to each other, say, the theory of ordered pairs of real numbers and two-dimensional Euclidean plane geometry. One theory commits us to points; the other commits us to pairs of reals. We may call these theories *mutually reducible*. In any given construction of the body of our theories about the world, only one of these reductions, at best, is likely to be sanctioned with ontological significance. Which should it be? Rudolf Carnap faces this problem in an acute form in the *Aufbau:* he finds the physical and the phenomenal realms to be mutually reducible. He recognizes that, once reducibility relations are established formally, the philosophically interesting question of how to structure our knowledge on the basis of these relations remains. To resolve this problem, Carnap introduces "epistemic primacy"; the reduction of the physical to the phenomenal ought to be preferred, he thinks, because of the epistemic primacy of the phenomenal. I hold a rather different view of epistemic primacy, which would rank the physical as fundamental. But I concur in Carnap's judgment that the jungle of possible constructional systems of our knowledge is to be cleared by epistemological considerations. For Carnap and for me, these considerations are not linguistic, but in a broad sense scientific. Gottlieb errs because he attempts to introduce epistemic conditions into an essentially linguistic framework; his attempt to clarify the epistemic structure of our theories is doomed because, his criteria notwithstanding, epistemic structure and primacy are ultimately nonlinguistic.

I shall investigate the distinction between what can be reduced to what (the problem of *reducibility*) and what ought to be reduced to what (the problem of *primacy*) further in the following chapter. For now we can say that, in general, *T can be reduced* to *T'* just in case *T* is interpretable in *T'*, in the sense expounded in chapter four. *T ought to be reduced* to *T'*, then, just in case *T* can be reduced to *T'*, and some condition of primacy is fulfilled. The condition of primacy will be the norm we have been seeking, to distinguish formal from nonformal criteria of reduction. The condition must (1) be nonlinguistic and (2) take into account our empirical theories about knowledge acquisition. I have assumed that there must be some empirically scrutable relationship between the objects of knowledge and ourselves as knowers; any theory of knowledge which does not take such relations into account or which ignores the need for matter-of-factual relations between the knower and the known, must fail to provide a satisfying explanation of our knowledge. But what matter-of-factual relations obtain between our cognitive faculties and objects of knowledge is an empirical question, which we cannot settle here. What ought to be reduced to what, then, depends upon the content of our best empirical theories concerning our cognitive capacities.

To return to neo-Pythagoreanism, we are reluctant to endow reductions to arithmetic with ontological significance because our knowledge of arithmetic is problematic. We stand in no empirically scrutable relationship, it seems, with the objects to which number theory ostensibly commits us. The knowledge we have of geographical topics, for example, is much more readily explicable. To reduce an empirical theory to a theory committing us only to abstract objects is surely to sacrifice epistemology on the altar of economy. We ought to be trying to perform reductions in the other direction, of theories with ostensible commitments to abstract entities to theories without such commitments. Where we are concerned with solely abstract theories, however, epistemological considerations fail to tell us anything so definite. Reducibility establishes a relative proximity relation, from an epistemological point of view; which of these relations will ultimately be of use in explicating the presently problematic knowledge we have of abstract entities, however, only the success of a reduction of the sort I have been recommending will tell.

We need not fear, therefore, that the Löwenheim-Skolem theorem undermines a linguistic approach to reduction. That the account accepts some peculiar reductions does no harm, so long as we have grounds for saying that these reductions are uninteresting on another level. The class of reductions that are formally acceptable is larger than the class of reductions that have ontological significance in the final construction of our knowledge; the problematic reductions sanctioned by the Löwenheim-Skolem theorem and its variants fall somewhere within this difference.

8 Interpretation and Ontology

Philosophers have long thought it fashionable to divide the fundamental question of ontology — What is there? — into two separate questions. Traditional metaphysics splits ontology into the study of particulars and universals, and so asks, What particulars are there? and What universals are there? Rudolf Carnap divides ontological issues into internal and external questions of existence, and Quine insists that we ask first, What does a theory say there is? and then proceed to the broader question, What theories ought we adopt? In this chapter I shall argue that such divisions of ontology are on the right track, though they have not been demarcated very clearly. I shall propose a new pair of questions which together enable us to make sense of the traditional project of ontology.

1. A Criterion of Ontological Commitment

Quine splits What is there? into two questions. One of them, What theories ought we adopt?, philosophers can treat only in a very general way, since we adopt theories for a wide variety of reasons, varying according to subject matter. What physical theory we should adopt, for example, is properly a question for the physicist to decide; which account of the French Revolution we should accept is best adjudicated by the historian. We should not be surprised, then, that Quine directs most of his attention to the other question, What does a theory say that there is?, for this seems amenable to philosophical treatment.

The philosopher interested in answering this first — particularly philosophical — question of ontology must take on the task of attempting to formulate an adequate criterion of ontological commitment, for a theory's ontological commitments correspond precisely to what the theory says there is. But it is important to remember that such a criterion does not by itself provide a solution to ontological problems; it does not tell us what there is, but only what some theory *says* there is.[1] We can summarize quite briefly Quine's famous criterion for ontological commitment: "to be is to be a value of a

1. W. V. Quine, *Word and Object* (Cambridge, Mass.: MIT Press, 1960), p. 243n. See "Carnap's Views on Ontology," in *The Ways of Paradox and Other Essays* (Cambridge, Mass.: Harvard, 1976): 203–211, pp. 203–4.

variable."[2] This formulation, however, does not make the dependence upon a theory explicit; Quine directs himself more to the point, perhaps, in saying, "to be assumed as an entity is, purely and simply, to be reckoned as the value of a variable."[3]

We can see from this formulation that, for Quine, ontological commitment has both syntactic and semantic aspects. Semantically, the criterion indicates that the assignment of values to variables of a theory carries particular ontological import; syntactically, it tells us that quantification is the locus of commitment. I shall examine both the syntactic and the semantic sides of Quine's criterion, and attempt to sharpen it as a tool for the clarification of ontology. Let us turn first to the syntactic aspects of the criterion.

Quine tells us that quantification is crucial to the determination of the ontological commitments of a theory, but this answer is very general; if we construe a theory as a logically closed set of sentences, then any theorem entails infinitely many others that are quantificational in form. Is there any way of sorting the interesting from the uninteresting quantificational formulas in this infinite collection?

We might guess that sentences with significance for questions of ontology and ontological commitment have existential quantifiers in them. In fact, I shall argue, we may be more specific: statements with initial existential quantifier strings constitute the locus of the ontological commitments of a theory.[4] This, I take it, is the insight that finds expression in the criterion proposed by Alonzo Church and others: that a theory T is ontologically committed to M's if and only if '$(\exists x)$ (Mx)' is a theorem of T.[5] Quine himself sometimes places the entire burden of ontic commitment upon the existential quantifier:

> We can very easily involve ourselves in ontological commitments by saying, for example, that *there is some-*

2. Quine, "A Logistical Approach to the Ontological Problem," in *The Ways of Paradox*; 197–202, p. 199.

3. Quine, "On What There Is," in *From a Logical Point of View* (New York: Harper & Row, 1961): 1–19, p. 13.

4. Vacuous quantification fails to expand the expressive power of a theory and makes the arguments that follow much less elegant, though no less valid. I shall therefore exclude vacuous quantification as ill formed.

5. See Alonzo Church, "Symposium: Ontological Commitment," *Journal of Philosophy*, LV (1958): 1008–1014; Jack C. Carloye, "Ontological Commitment and Semantics," *Methodology of Science*, X (1977): 169–176.

thing (bound variable) which red houses and sunsets have in common; or that *there is something* which is a prime number larger than a million. But this is, essentially, the *only* way we can involve ourselves in ontological commitments: by our use of bound variables.[6]

Though Quine here emphasizes the role of bound variables in general, his examples are all existential quantifications. In other passages as well, his examples are all existential: we commit ourselves ontologically by saying that *"there are* black swans, that *there is* a mountain more than 8800 meters high, and that *there are* prime numbers above a hundred."[7] More conclusively, Quine's arguments for his criterion, brief though they are, tend to turn on existential quantification in particular, rather than on quantification in general:

> To insist on the correctness of the criterion in this application is, indeed, merely to say that no distinction is being drawn between the 'there are' of 'there are universals', 'there are unicorns', 'there are hippopotami', and the 'there are' of '$(\exists x)$', 'there are entities such that'.[8]

Finally, in "Existence and Quantification," Quine admits that the existential quantifier is the bearer of ontic commitment:

> In general we may say that an expression is used in a theory as naming if and only if the existentially quantified identity built on that expression is true according to the theory. . . .

> It is the existential quantifier, not the *"a"* itself, that carries existential import. This is just what existential quantification is for, of course. It is a logically regimented rendering of the "there is" idiom.[9]

We may plausibly interpret Quine, then, as holding that the bearer of ontological commitment is the existential quantifier. I shall contend, furthermore, that Quine is essentially correct to do so. His chief argument for the view appears to be that

6. Quine, "On What There Is," p. 12.

7. "Carnap's Views on Ontology," p. 205.

8. "Logic and the Reification of Universals," in *From a Logical Point of View* (New York: Harper & Row, 1961): 102–129, p. 105.

9. Quine, "Existence and Quantification," in *Ontological Relativity and Other Essays* (New York: Columbia, 1969): 91–113, p. 94.

the existential quantifier, by design, functions to ascribe existence. There is thus a certain naturalness to taking the existential quantifier as imputing existence, as its very name suggests.

Nevertheless, many philosophers have held that questions of ontological commitment cannot be treated in terms of existential quantification alone. Many of these have stressed the significance of names, but if Quine is correct that to take an expression as a name is to be willing to quantify with respect to it, this amounts to no major disagreement. I shall therefore direct my attention to refuting the contention that other quantified statements carry ontological commitment. Consider the following sentences of a formalized theory T:

$$(1) \qquad (x)\,(\exists y)\,(Fxy)$$

$$(2) \qquad (x)\,(y)\,(x = y)$$

$$(3) \qquad (x)\,(\exists y)\,(x = y)$$

$$(4) \qquad (\exists x)\,(x = x)$$

One might argue that each of these sentences has ontological import. The first, though not existential in a direct way, is surely relevant to what T says exists; the presence of the existential quantifier forces the statement to have some ontological commitment or signficance, we might think, just as much as does '$(\exists x)\,(Mx)$'.[10] Statement (2), similarly, places a severe restriction on what exists and so seems highly relevant to ontology, though it contains no existential quantifiers at all. In contrast, statement (3) has the same quantificational form as (1), but is logically valid, and seems to carry no ontological import: it has roughly the significance of the law of identity. Thus we might decide that the ontic significance of a sentence cannot be read from its quantificational structure alone, much less the structure of only its existential quantifiers. Much more about the content of the statements may seem relevant to questions concerning what exists.

I take it that one who advances these arguments would agree with me that (4) does have ontic significance, at least in

---

10. See Michael Dummett, *Frege: Philosophy of Language* (London: Harper & Row, 1973), p. 476. Statement (1) is Dummett's example; whether he intends it against limiting ontological concern to existential quantification, or to initial existential quantification, is not clear. Parenthetical page references to Dummett will be to this book.

part by virtue of its existential quantifier. The formula is in fact valid in standard quantification theory and marks that system as exclusive, ruling out the null domain. Bertrand Russell recognized that in the system of *Principia Mathematica* it can be proved that there is at least one object in the universe; (4) is a theorem that implies this. We may translate (4) as 'There is something', which is about as vague an ontological commitment as we might hope to achieve. It is an ontological commitment nonetheless. Inclusive logics have been developed to exclude such an ontological assumption from the realm of logic where, as Russell felt, no such presupposition belongs.

I claim that there is a substantial difference between (4) and (1)–(3), based upon the initial existential quantification found only in (4). The difference may be spelled out quite simply: only (4) rules out a null domain. It cannot be satisfied in the null domain because it requires that there be objects over which we can quantify. (1), (2), and (3), in contrast, make no such requirement; in the most plausible inclusive logics, and in fact, in any inclusive logic I know of, they would come out true. I am suggesting, therefore, that *we may construe no statement as carrying ontological commitment which comes out true on the null domain.* If a sentence may come out true even if nothing at all exists, then clearly the sentence does not involve a commitment to anything. It may have some "ontological import" in the sense that it helps to imply theorems that do have initial existential quantifiers, but it does not have any ontological force in its own right. Any sentence with any content, after all, is relevant to questions of existence in the broadest sense, for it delimits the class of models that satisfy whatever theory is at hand. But nothing distinguishes (1) or (2) from a sentence such as

$$(5) \qquad (x)\,(Fx \supset Gx)$$

which clearly has no commitment to the existence of anything. Even sentences such as (5) have some sort of ontic bearing, for, if (5) is true, for example, there can be nothing that is an F yet not a G. The sentence does limit the models satisfying whatever theory it calls home, but does not thereby involve any ontological commitment.

If we accept the contention that any statement carrying ontological commitment must come out false on the null domain, we can see that sentences with initial existential quantifier strings are the locus of ontological commitment from a syntactic point of view; they are the only sentences that come out false when there are no objects in the universe of discourse.[11] Not only do all currently developed inclusive logics have this character, but any reasonable inclusive logic must make sentences with initial strings of existential quantifiers false on the empty domain. Because of the interdefinability of the universal and existential quantifiers, we are forced to choose, on pain of inconsistency, whether to make all sentences with initial universal quantifiers false, or all sentences with initial existential quantifiers false. We choose the existential quantifiers because of their intuitive significance as representing existence. Thus, if nothing at all exists, should we reject as false '$(\exists x) (x = x)$' or '$(x) (x = x)$'? The former says that something exists; the latter says that everything is self-identical. Clearly we should choose to make the claim that something exists false, since in point of fact, nothing does exist in the empty domain. Thus Quine's appeal to our intuitive renderings of the quantifiers, and to our intentions concerning their interpretation, takes on greater force. In considering a semantics for the null domain we must give one quantifier or the other existential significance; that this should be the existential quantifier we justify by an appeal to our intended interpretations and to the interpretations the quantifiers in fact receive in exclusive logic. But the assertion that one quantifier or the other must be endowed with ontic significance we justify by the demands of a semantics for the empty universe, not by an appeal to intuitions or intentions. We may restrict our attention to *initial* existential quantification because existential quantifiers occurring after universal ones have at best a conditional commitment, as in (1), and sometimes, as in (3), have no commitment at all. Thus a consideration of the empty domain, though it may seem to be "much ado about nothing," provides a key for the formulation of a syntactic criterion of ontological commitment.

The formulation of a semantic criterion is more difficult. Syntactically we may say that, if a theory has a theorem of the form '$(\exists x) (Mx)$', it is ontologically committed to M's. But

11. See, e.g., A. Mostowski, "On the Rules of Proof in the Pure Functional Calculus of the First Order," *Journal of Symbolic Logic*, XVI (1951): 107–111; T. Hailperin, "Quantification Theory and Empty Individual Domains," *Journal of Symbolic Logic*, XVIII (1953): 197–200; Quine, "Quantification and the Empty Domain," reprinted in *Selected Logic Papers* (New York: Random House, 1966): 220–223.

what are M's? As a syntactic unit, the theory gives us no information about this. To tell what M's are, we need to refer to the interpretation of the theory, that is, to its semantics. As an uninterpreted theory form, it tells us nothing about what the objects of the theory are supposed to be.

What is an interpretation of a theory? Unfortunately, there is no clear answer on which philosophers have reached a consensus. One conception of an interpretation is that it assigns an object to each singular term of the theory and a set of n-tuples of objects to each n-ary predicate of the theory. This conception of interpretation is fostered by the formal depiction of a theory's semantics, for we tend to invoke functions that do just this. But, in this respect, the formalism may be misleading.[12] In any case, if we imagine interpretation as a direct and unambiguous link between the expressions of the theory and extralinguistic objects, we will have difficulty in appreciating the force of Quine's criterion. If we already have a clearly defined conception of the universe of the theory, what is the point of asking questions about ontological commitment?

Quine wavers between conceiving of a theory as uninterpreted and as interpreted, even in the same passage. He occasionally identifies the ontology of a theory with its ontological commitments (thus "the ontology of a theory is a question of what the assertions say or imply that there is," and "given a theory, one philosophically interesting aspect of it into which we can inquire is its ontology: what entities are the variables of quantification to range over if the theory is to hold true?"[13]), but at times Quine distinguishes ontology from ontological commitment:

> The ontology is the range of the variables. Each of the various reinterpretations of the range (while keeping the interpretations of the predicates fixed) might be compatible with the theory. But the theory is ontically *committed* to an object only if that object is common to all those ranges. And the theory is ontically committed to 'objects

---

12. See Jeffrey Sicha, "Logic: The Fundamentals of a Sellarisian Theory," in Joseph C. Pitt, ed., *The Philosophy of Wilfrid Sellars: Queries and Extensions* (Boston: Reidel, 1978): 257–286. See also Robert Kraut, "Indiscernibility and Ontology," *Synthese*, XLIV (1980): 113–135.

13. "Ontology and Ideology," *Philosophical Studies*, II (1951): 11–15, p. 14.

of such and such kind', say dogs, just in case each of those ranges contains some dog or other.[14]

If an interpreted theory comes with its own specified universe, in the sense that there is a direct link between the expressions of the theory and some extralinguistic objects, ontology must be a trivial matter: the ontology of a theory is just the collection of objects so linked with expressions of the theory. Ontological commitment, Quine appears to say, is a more complicated issue. In explaining commitment, however, Quine speaks of a theory reinterpreted with different ranges. But, if a theory comes with its universe specified, how can we speak of the theory as identical while undergoing the reinterpretations? If specifying a universe is an integral part of specifying a theory, then any change in the range of the variables changes the theory.

Quine, we may note, distinguishes between a commitment to an entity and a commitment to entities of a certain sort. "To be assumed as an entity is . . . to be reckoned as the value of a variable" suggests that ontological commitment is a relation between a theory and an entity. But a theory may be committed to dogs, though not to any particular dogs; no entity stands in the relation of ontological commitment to the theory, but it is absurd to hold that the theory is *ipso facto* free of commitment.[15] Quine thus needs a separate clause to handle commitments to objects of a certain kind—we may call them *generic* commitments—which do not involve commitments to any particular objects. Since Quine holds that names can be eliminated from theories, most theories will have no commitments to individuals; at best we can determine models up to isomorphism. Thus, given Quine's view of theories and names, generic commitments are primary.

We may also recognize another departure from the early formulations of the criterion. "To be is to be a value of a variable" asserts that we need to examine what we take as values of our variables to determine the ontological commitments of a theory. Quine now appears to take this as an indication of the ontology of a theory; the determination of ontological commitment requires a comparison of possible universes, a comparison across models, which requires a consideration of

14. "Reply to Hintikka," in Donald Davidson and Jaakko Hintikka, eds., *Words and Objections* (Boston: Reidel, 1969): 312–315, p. 315.

15. See Leslie Stevenson, "On What Sorts of Thing There Are," *Mind*, LXXXV (1976): 503–521, p. 507.

a variety of different ontologies for the same theory. This may introduce an element of intensionality into the notion of commitment;[16] the intensionality involved, however, is minimal, going no further than the notion of validity of an argument form in requiring comparisons across models. Moreover, though Quine prefers to think of commitment as belonging to the theory of reference rather than to the theory of meaning,[17] he appears to recognize the intensionality of ontic commitment. The modality of many formulations of the criterion is striking: a theory is committed to entities which "must be counted among the values of the variables," "over which our variables of quantification have to range," and which are "needed among the values of the bound variables" in order to make the statements of the theory true.[18]

Suppose that we have a first-order theory T, which has a theorem '$(\exists x) (Mx)$', where M's are informally understood to be molecules. In each model of the theory, the extension of M is nonempty; so some elements of the universe on each model must be molecules. We say, in such a case, that T is ontologically committed to molecules. In general, the ontological commitments of the theory, on this approach, correspond precisely to those sanctioned by the syntactic criterion. There will be M's in every model of a theory just in case '$(\exists x)$ (Mx)' is a theorem.

Quine, however, has reason to reject this interpretation of the semantic aspects of his criterion of ontological commitment. He advocates both a first-order view of theories and the centrality of nondenumerable domains for the project of ontology. Given our current view of his criterion, these views contradict each other. Consider set theory, where we have Cantor's theorem asserting the existence of uncountably many sets. Quine, quite naturally, holds that set theory is committed to nondenumerably many sets. But we know by the Löwenheim-Skolem theorem that set theory is in fact satisfiable in a countable domain; Skolem-paradoxically, even Cantor's theorem is satisfiable on a denumerable domain. We

16. See R. L. Cartwright," Ontology and the Theory of Meaning," *Philosophy of Science*, XXI (1954): 316–325; Beverly Robbins, "Ontology and the Heirarchy of Languages," *Philosophical Review*, LXVII (1958): 531–537; Michael Jubien, "The Intensionality of Ontological Commitment," *Noûs*, VI (1972): 378–387.

17. "Ontology and Ideology," p. 15.

18. "Logic and the Reification of Universals," p. 103; "Carnap's Views on Ontology," p. 205; see also "Logic and the Reification of Universals," p. 108.

do not need, therefore, an uncountable universe to make the assertions of set theory come out true. Since the same holds true for any first-order theory, we are led to the conclusion that no theory can be committed ontologically to anything but a countable domain. But this violates Quine's contention that uncountably infinite universes are the chief sources of ontology's interest.

Quine does not speak of commitments to a given cardinality of objects in a domain, but we can extrapolate the criterion quite easily. If in every model of T there is at least one M, we say that T is ontically committed to M's. If there are at least two M's in each model of T, we can say that T carries a commitment to at least two M's; in general, T is committed to n M's just in case there are at least n M's in every model of T. But then, since any first-order theory has a countable model (or a finite one), no such theory can carry ontic commitment to anything more than a countable universe.

The key to Quine's response, and to his view of the semantic aspects of his criterion, is his demand for the specification of a proxy function. A proxy function is needed to pare the universe down to denumerable size in a legitimate way; clearly Quine is thinking of a theory as coming with an already specified domain, for otherwise there would be no initial domain to pare down. But, since we have an intended universe, of what use is the criterion? We start with the intended domain, but recognize by way of Quine's criterion that some of these objects are not needed to ensure the truth of the theory. We may dispense with these objects, but only if we can specify a proxy function, or meet Quine's related demands concerning what Richard Grandy has called "ontological destruction."[19] Quine's requirements succeed from a technical point of view in blocking the conclusion that we can never be committed by a first-order theory to anything more than a countable universe; their independent motivation, however, is obscure. But, if the specification of an ontology (i.e., an intended universe) is integral to the specification of a theory, Quine's demands make sense. Consider two theories T and T'; T we present with an intended universe, some of which is superfluous. T' is identical with T, except that the superfluous objects in the domain of T have been dropped from the ontology of the theory. How can we characterize the universe of T'? If we cannot specify that universe

19. See "On What There Need Not Be," *Journal of Philosophy*, LXVI (1969), 809–811; Quine, "Ontological Relativity," in *Ontological Relativity and Other Essays*: 26–68, p. 68.

in an acceptable way, we cannot specify what theory it is we are talking about, for we are assuming that specifying the universe is integral to specifying the theory. Though we can pare down the size of an uncountable domain by way of the Löwenheim-Skolem theorem, we cannot characterize the resulting universe in a sense that would satisfy Quine; we cannot specify which objects are dropped and which are retained in the model.

Quine is thinking, then, of a theory as interpreted, in the sense that its predicates have intuitive meanings assigned to them, and the theory itself is assigned an intended universe characterized in terms of the resources of the metalanguage. The universe is fixed, in the sense that its specification is integral to the specification of the theory; the criterion of ontological commitment emerges as a way of indicating when we might be able to dispense with a portion of the intended domain, though this operation is constrained by the proxy-function requirement. Since this requirement raises problems on other grounds, as we have seen in the previous chapter, Quine's position seems unsatisfying. But deeper problems arise for the criterion: how do we go about specifying intended interpretations and domains? What justifies the invocation of the resources of the metalanguage in speaking about acceptable ways of specifying a universe? Finally, how does this conception relate to ontological reduction?

2. Ontological Commitment and Reduction

We are now in a position to see the full force of an objection I am about to raise against Quine. His criterion for ontological commitment focuses on quantificational sentences and, in particular, on sentences with initial existential quantifier strings, to determine the ontological commitments of a theory. To simplify, we seem to have reached the position that sentences of the form '$(\exists x)(Mx)$' carry ontological commitment to M's.

But Quine also stresses the significance of reduction as a technical and philosophical tool. He takes pains to work out a reasonable criterion of ontological reduction, and emphasizes the utility of this technique in ridding us of problems arising from needless verbal usages.[20] One such problem Quine envisages is the commitment to unsavory entities in one's on-

20. See 'Ontological Reduction and the World of Numbers," in *The Ways of Paradox:* 212–220; "Ontological Relativity"; also *Word and Object,* pp. 260–1.

tology: he applauds Carnap's reduction of impure numbers of temperature to pure numbers, freeing us from any commitment to the peculiar impure numbers. Similarly, Quine cheers Russell's analysis of sentences which, as we would now say, contain nondenoting singular terms, for it shows that we do not need to assume obscure entities such as "meanings" or "subsisting beings" in order to account for the truth values of such sentences.

For the sake of clarity, let us focus on the reduction of number theory to set theory, say ZF. Quine clearly believes that the reduction demonstrates that we need not be committed to numbers, but at most to sets alone.[21] We nevertheless retain arithmetic, continuing to accept and use sentences of the form '$(\exists x)(Mx)$', where 'M' represents a number-theoretic predicate such as 'is a prime number', or even 'is a number'. These sentences, according to Quine's criterion, commit us to the existence of numbers. But Quine claims that, since number theory can be reduced to set theory, we can forsake such commitments. How? Must we assume that Quine's criterion for ontological commitment is not sufficient for commitment after all?

This is, of course, a general problem. A reduced theory may force upon us considerable ontological commitments, by the criterion as we have so far developed it. Nevertheless, Quine asserts that these commitments may be abandoned as a result of the reduction. He comes close to recognizing this difficulty when he observes:

> . . . when we say that some zoölogical species are cross-fertile we are committing ourselves to recognizing as entities the several species themselves, abstract though they are. We remain so committed at least until we devise some way of so paraphrasing the statement as to show that the seeming reference to species on the part of our bound variable was an avoidable manner of speaking.[22]

But if we retain the reduced theory and if Quine's criterion is a necessary and sufficient condition for ontological commitment, the eliminability of a mode of discourse appears to be irrelevant. Thus reduction would appear to have no ontological significance after all. If we are to avoid this conclusion,

21. See "A Logistical Approach to the Ontological Problem," p. 201.

22. Quine, "On What There Is," p. 13.

either we must reject Quine's criterion as failing to be both necessary and sufficient, or we must insist that reduced theories are no longer accepted in a way that forces us to take their ontological commitments seriously. The reduction, we might say, gives us reason to reject number theory in our account of the world; we can forsake its commitments because we can forsake the theory altogether. "Explication is elimination," Quine says,[23] by explicating number theory in terms of set theory, we might say, we have eliminated not only numbers in favor of sets, but the theory of numbers in favor of the theory of sets as well.

Unfortunately, this alternative is highly counterintuitive. We have not given up arithmetic as a result of the aforementioned reduction. We all use it frequently, in fact, and we believe arithmetical statements to be true. The situation might be different if we were to speak of Newtonian mechanics, for in that case we could argue that the theory is used merely as an approximation to the more complex Einsteinian theory for reasons of convenience; we use Newton's theory without believing it to be true. Thus we might use a theory without accepting it, in the strict sense of the term. But we hold number-theoretic theorems to be true, not merely approximations to the truth which are useful for the sake of convenience. We still accept arithmetic, therefore, in spite of the existence of set-theoretic accounts of number.

But though we do still accept the reduced theory, we might argue that we no longer need to accept it. We can say everything we want to say without accepting number theory; though we are ontologically committed to numbers because we persist in accepting the theory, we do not need to be. A persuasive metaphysician might therefore attempt to move us from our acceptance of arithmetic, and reform us from these needless usages with their attendant but needless commitments. He might charge that we need to reform our ordinary language to avoid philosophically objectionable commitments. Though this strategy might be appropriate in certain circumstances, there seems little chance that our metaphysician will persuade us to surrender our employment of arithmetic.

A crafty metaphysician might respond that Quine's criterion tells us what a theory says there is; the other question of ontology is not What theories ought we adopt? but rather What theories might we adopt, and still provide an adequate account of things? We can introduce the notion of necessity,

---

23. *Word and Object*, p. 261.

of needing to adopt a theory or assume the existence of a class of objects, into the other half of ontology. We need not be committed to numbers, on this approach, because we do not need to employ number theory in painting our general portrait of the world. But reduction appears to be saying something quite different about theory acceptance. When we see that arithmetic can be reduced to set theory, we do not reject arithmetic, but instead recognize that, in accepting set theory, we are already in effect accepting arithmetic. Thus we are not shown that we do, or can, or must reject the theory of numbers; we are shown that we need do nothing more than accept set theory in order to accept number theory. Charles Chihara and Otto Chateaubriand use this insight to argue that reduction does not cancel ontological commitment. The reduction of number theory to set theory, on their account, shows only that set theory is committed to numbers every bit as much as arithmetic itself. They conclude that we ought to take the criterion seriously, but reject as ontologically useless the notion of reduction.[24] But in accepting set theory, we are already, in effect, accepting number theory; we thus accept numbers, but not as distinct from sets. Though set theory may in some sense commit us to numbers, the reduction shows us that such a commitment is no different from a commitment to sets. Set theory does not commit us to two distinct realms, but only to sets; no more need be assumed as numbers than that.

A deeper problem emerges as well. Suppose that we have two theories we accept, each of which reduces to the other, as occurs frequently in mathematical contexts. Such theories, we may say, are *mutually reducible*. How do we account for these theories? It would seem that, if a reduction demonstrates that we need not accept the reduced theory, we do not need to accept either of these theories. But suppose that, as it happens, we must adopt one or the other. So far, our reformulated second question of ontology implies that we are not committed to the ontologies of mutually reducible theories at all, since, given any such theory, there is another to which it reduces. Carnap, for example, finds that the physical and phenomenal realms are mutually reducible, but does not conclude that we have no ontological commitment to either realm; the problem becomes, Which of the reducibility rela-

24. See Chihara, *Ontology and the Vicious Circle Principle* (Ithaca: N.Y.: Cornell, 1973), pp. 129, 133; Chateaubriand, *Ontic Commitment, Ontological Reduction, and Ontology* (Ph.D. dissertation, University of California at Berkeley, 1971), pp. 148–9.

tions ought we to take seriously from an ontological point of view? Surely mutual reducibility does not allow us to dispense with questions of ontological commitment altogether.

We cannot, therefore, insist that reduced theories are not accepted in a way that forces us to take their ontological commitments seriously. The only alternative, however, is to say that Quine's criterion is not both necessary and sufficient for ontological commitment. But we have noted that the notion of an interpretation of a theory, though not very clear in general, is needed to make sense of Quine's criterion from a semantical point of view. Though sentences such as '$(\exists x)(Mx)$' commit us to the existence of M's, on a syntactic view of the criterion, there remains the question of what M's are. And this can be answered only if we have in mind some interpretation of the formalized theory. So long as we view this interpretation as fixed, or clearly defined, independent of reducibility relations, we encounter problems, particularly when we try to explain how reduction can have any ontological impact. Thus, if we have some independent account of what M's are, the theory at hand is committed to those objects, and reducibility relations are beside the point. Quine, therefore, denies that there is a clear and independent concept of the interpretation of a theory. Though his primary motivations may be elsewhere, Quine presents his doctrine of "ontological relativity," that "reference is nonsense except relative to a coordinate system."[25] He notes that it is impossible to specify, within a theory, what model we intend for the theory to have. Thus the notion of an intended model, upon which the criterion is based, may be misleading; we can specify our intentions only in the metalanguage. But the terms of the metalanguage suffer from the same problems as those of the object language. Which model of the metalanguage do we intend? The answer, apparently, can be given only in the metametalanguage, and so on. To break this regress, we generally take the metalanguage at face value, not asking about its intended interpretation. We assume that we share enough of an understanding of our intentions in using it to get by. Thus Haskell Curry refers to a broad, shared metalanguage as the *U-language*,[26] the language that we actually *use*: this is the language that provides the frame of ref-

25. "Ontological Relativity," p. 48. Hereafter, parenthetical page references to Quine will be to this paper, unless noted otherwise.

26. *Foundations of Mathematical Logic* (New York: Dover, 1977), pp. 28–32.

erence relative to which we interpret other theories. Quine seeks to avoid the difficulty concerning the seeming incompatibility of reduction and his criterion of ontological commitment by arguing that we cannot speak of commitments in an absolute sense. We must think of a theory's commitments as relative to the background language in which the interpretation of the theory is given.

Quine characterizes his thesis of ontological relativity as the assertion that "it makes no sense to say what the objects of a theory are beyond saying how to interpret or reinterpret that theory in another" (50). Thus, "what makes sense is to say not what the objects of a theory are, absolutely speaking, but how one theory of objects is interpretable or reinterpretable in another" (50). There is therefore no difference, Quine says, between "specifying a universe of discourse—the range of the variables of quantification—and *reducing* that universe to some other" (43–4). Consequently, reduction serves to interpret, or reinterpret, the reduced theory. When we take arithmetic at face value, for example, we interpret it in the U-language as being about numbers. When we reduce arithmetic to set theory, however, we reinterpret the theory as being about sets, at least if we take that theory seriously from the perspective of ontology. The ontological commitment to numbers we thus show to be only apparent. It is a commitment relative to our background language. When we choose to talk in the U-language in terms of sets rather than numbers, we interpret number theory as a theory about sets in certain of their guises. To say what the objects of a theory are turns out to be to say how reference to those objects can be eliminated in favor of reference to something else. In attempting to deal with the question of what there is, then, we must analyze what there is *not*. Ontological relativity reconciles Quine's criterion with his emphasis on ontological reduction, by leading us to take less seriously his criterion of ontological commitment. To speak in terms of the ontological commitments of a theory *T*, according to the ontological-relativity thesis, is a mistake: we ought to speak of the commitments of *T* relative to some background language *L*.

Though the ontological-relativity doctrine resolves the tension between Quine's criterion of ontological commitment and his emphasis on reduction, it leaves many questions unanswered. What is the nature of the background language? What happens in that language when we decide, for example, to reinterpret number theory as being about sets? Given a set of interpretability relations, which do we take seriously from an ontological point of view? When we are faced with mutually reducible theories, how may we decide which theory ought to be reduced to which?

3. A Reformulation of Ontological Questions

These questions bring us to the heart of problems concerning the nature of ontology. I shall not attempt to answer all of them here. Instead, I shall focus on a bit of uneasiness which Quine's appeal to ontological relativity fails to satisfy. If we ask not what the ontic commitments of a theory are, but, always, what the commitments are relative to a background language, we find that no answers can be given unless we have a full account of the background language. And this, apparently, can be given only if we already know what we intend to interpret as what. To take an example, we may ask about the commitments of number theory relative to the U-language. These can be determined only if we know to what theory, if any, number theory is to be reduced in our over-all theory of the world. Questions about ontological commitments thus become entwined with questions concerning which reductions we ought to take as ontologically interesting. Until that problem can be solved, it makes no sense to speak of commitments in terms of our U-language. But in fact commitments, or seeming commitments, in terms of the U-language generally motivate attempts at ontological reduction. Number theory, from a naive point of view, commits us to abstract entities; that is why we become worried about the epistemology of number theory in the first place. In short, the above questions about the role of the background language are crucial to Quine's criterion and are also very difficult to answer. I shall propose a new pair of questions to elucidate the nature of ontology, which do not take for granted a full theory of how our U-language functions.

The quantificational structure of a theory gives us the *prima facie* ontological commitments of the theory. These commitments are rebuttable in principle, for we can show that the given theory can be reduced to some other theory without the same commitments. We can thus speak of the commitments of a theory in a virtually absolute sense, without explicitly specifying a frame of reference. A syntactic consideration of the initially existentially quantified sentences of a theory, for example, provides a clear explication of what the theory commits us to, though it fails to provide the information we regard as most interesting. To say more, we need to interpret the theory concerned, and this, as we have seen, raises difficulties. We need a background language in terms of which we can interpret the original theory. But, typically, we do have some intuitive interpretation of a theory in mind in the U-language before we raise any question of reducibility. Number theory, to take an example, is about numbers; set theory concerns sets; the theory of metric spaces concerns metric spaces, etc. Although Quine is correct to insist that we need some background language to do any interpreting of a theory, we naively interpret our theories in the U-language, without bothering about any questions of reducibility, interpretability, etc. Thus I prefer to say that number theory forces a *prima facie* commitment to numbers; set theory, a *prima facie* commitment to sets, and so forth. We can then ask about what numbers, sets, etc., really are. The U-language, from this point of view, gives us only minimal information about the commitments of the theory. We may be able to tell that number theory is committed to numbers, and *a fortiori* to abstract entities; to say any more, however, we must consider issues surrounding reduction.

The commitments that a theory forces upon us, by virtue of its quantificational structure and its naive interpretation in the U-language, I shall call the *ostensible commitments* of that theory. Arithmetic thus has an ostensible commitment to numbers, set theory an ostensible commitment to sets. These commitments do not possess ultimate philosophical significance, for they are only *prima facie* commitments; they can be refuted. We may know that the theory concerned reduces to another theory without any such commitment. Reduction has ontological significance because it can show that the ostensible commitments of a theory are *only* ostensible and need not be taken seriously from the point of view of ontology. The *reducibility* of a theory to another involving other commitments, then, amounts to the *refutability* of the ostensible commitments of the reduced theory. Ostensible commitments are thus refutable in two senses. They are refutable *in principle* in that they are *prima facie* in character; it is always possible that we might adopt a theory to which the theory concerned reduces. They are refutable *in fact* when we actually have such a reduction of the theory to some other theory having different commitments, which we also accept, in hand.

Recognizing the *prima facie* character of the ostensible commitments of a theory leads us to diverge from Quine in a significant way. He is emphatic that the word 'exists', or the phrase 'there is', must be taken as univocal throughout discourse. His arguments for the criterion of ontological commitment assume that these expressions, as well as '($\exists x$)', have a single sense. But, if the line of thought I am pursuing is correct, we must distinguish two senses of existential expressions: one an ostensible, or everyday sense, and the other a special, philosophically interesting sense. We all believe that arithmetic is true; just as clearly, arithmetic quantifies over numbers. Thus we all have an ostensible commitment to numbers. If we are asked, "Are there numbers?" the easy answer is, "Of course, there are numbers"—after all, infinitely many of them are prime—but this is unlikely to satisfy the philosopher interested in ontology. He might think that though in some truistic sense we can say that there are numbers, there really are no such things at all. The philosopher, in investigating ontology, has an interest in this sort of existence claim. As Wilfrid Sellars has expressed the distinction,

> In one sense of 'exist' it is beyond question that both minds and bodies exist; in another the question whether minds or bodies or either or neither exist is the crux of a legitimate and intricate philosophical puzzle—the Mind-Body problem. Accordingly, the philosopher, after agreeing with common sense that there are both minds and bodies, goes on to ask whether mental facts are "reducible" to physical facts, or vice versa, or whether both are "reducible" to facts which are neither.[27]

We may, in Sellarsian fashion, distinguish these two questions as Are there K's?—which, most frequently, permits of a truistic answer, "of course" or "of course not"—and Are there *really* K's? where the 'really' signifies that a philosophical point is being made. Questions of the first sort, which I have called questions of ostensible commitment, can be answered by examining quantification and, in particular, initial existential quantification, together with an intuitive, or naive interpretation of the theory in the U-language. There is a point to such questions; they are not foolish, though they are not usually philosophically interesting. If we ask in this sense, Are there ghosts?, we ask whether any of the theories we accept about the world quantify over ghosts. Though this

27. "Mind, Meaning, and Behavior," *Philosophical Studies*, III (1952): 83–95, p. 83; see *Naturalism and Ontology* (Reseda, Calif.: Ridgeview, 1979), p. 6.

distinction between senses of existence may be reminiscent of Rudolf Carnap's distinction between internal and external questions of existence, it is not the same distinction; we may ask questions of ostensible commitment with respect to ghosts, numbers, towns, in general or in particular. When we ask Are there *really* numbers? we do not ask whether or not we ought to adopt the framework of numbers, Carnap thinks, but rather whether the theory of numbers ought to be taken as basic in our conceptual scheme.

The claim that there are two senses of 'exists' is of course controversial. The tradition supporting this view goes back at least as far as Plato, who held that the Forms exist in a way dramatically different from that in which ordinary, temporal objects exist. Nevertheless, philosophers influenced by positivism have been skeptical of the meaningfulness of claims of "ultimate" existence and the like, and have regarded the "honorific" sense of 'exists' as a mere confusion.[28] Most often such philosophers have asserted that no one has ever given a precise sense to the peculiarly ontological sense of 'exists'. But in fact such a sense can be given; in large part, it *has* been given by the analysis I have developed of the concept of reduction.

A final implication of the distinction between the ostensible and real commitments of a theory is that existence, in an ontologically interesting sense, and the existential quantifier are not so closely linked as many philosophers, including Quine, have supposed. Quantification is intimately linked with the everyday sense of 'exists', which is roughly what we employ in asking about ostensible commitments. But it does not express what a philosopher means by existence in considering problems of ontology. Thus, to the extent that quantification tells us what there is, it does so in an ontologically uninteresting sense. The ostensible commitments of our theories are important even for the philosopher; they create the fabric of problems that the philosopher must face in coming to grips with ontological questions. Given that an accepted theory ostensibly commits us to entities of a certain kind, we may either grant that the ostensible commitment is an ontological, or real commitment, or, by way of reduction, refute the assumption of commitment by showing that our need for the objects is only apparent. Questions of ostensible

---

28. See William Alston, "Ontological Commitment, in Benacerraf and Putnam: 249–257, p. 251; Alan Ross Anderson, "Church on Ontological Commitment," *Journal of Philosophy*, LVI (1959): 448–452, pp. 451–2.

commitment, then, define the task of ontology, but do not constitute its chief subject matter.

The truly interesting question for ontology—What is there, really?—is a question of what we are to take as basic in our account of the world. One aspect of this issue, as Quine notes, goes beyond the realm of the philosopher, for the problem of what theories we ought to adopt must be answered by experts in specific disciplines. But the philosopher still has much to say; for, given a collection of theories that the specialists say ought to be adopted and given the ostensible commitments of these theories defined by their quantificational structure and by our naive view of the U-language, we may still ask what is to be reduced to what. Which theories should we take as basic, and which should we reduce to others? This we may in turn split into two questions, as I have argued in the previous chapter. To know what is to be reduced to what, we must ask first, What is reducible to what?—a question to which we can give a formally precise answer—and then, What ought to be reduced to what?, which is a far broader problem. The question of what *can* be reduced to what, I have said, is a question of *reducibility;* what *ought* to be reduced to what, in contrast, is a question of *primacy.* The problem of primacy is systematic, dealing with the large-scale explanatory structure of our discourse. The theories we declare to be basic will be those we understand as explaining why the objects assumed by the reduced theories behave in the ways they do according to those theories. To define a sharp concept of primacy, one would have to spell out precisely the nature of such explanatory relations. Unfortunately, this is far too large a task to be accomplished here. Nevertheless, we can formulate one criterion for making choices about our ultimate ontological commitments, which will constitute a part of a full account of primacy.

Given any collection of theories we accept about the world, there will be some subsets of the collection which contain theories to which (jointly) all other theories in the collection reduce, and which have no proper subsets having the same property. Let the set of theories we accept be W. Then there are subsets U_i of W such that every element of W reduces to some element of U_i, and no proper subset Z of U_i is such that, for every theory T in W, there is a theory in Z to which T reduces. The U_i we may call *possible bases* of our conceptual framework. We can give a technically precise, linguistic answer to the question of what the possible bases of our conceptual scheme are, for this is a problem belonging to the realm of reducibility. We move to a problem of primacy when we attempt to decide which of the possible bases of our framework we will employ for the actual construction of our knowledge, that is, for the construction we will take seriously from an ontological point of view. The ontological commitments of the theories of the basis in this construction we must recognize as real commitments; the others of the conceptual framework we may regard as merely ostensible. The U_i that we select as the foundation for our framework in this serious philosophical sense, we will call the *basis* of the conceptual scheme. From the point of view of ontology, then, the problem of what ought to be reduced to what becomes a problem of selecting a basis for the conceptual scheme we employ.

I have already said that a complete resolution of the problem of the selection of a basis for our conceptual scheme would require a full account of the nature of intertheoretic explanatory relations, particularly on levels more basic than those represented by reductive relations. But we can make a beginning at attacking this problem, and even formulate a criterion for what Quine calls "ontic decision." Benacerraf's dilemma—and our more general dilemma concerning the truth of theories involving ostensible commitments to abstract objects—arises from a tension between semantics and epistemology. The theories involved commit us, it appears, to objects that have no connection to our cognitive faculties: numbers, sets, and possibilities, for example. I have argued that the only solution to this difficulty is to reduce the theories forcing such problematic commitments to theories that do not commit us to abstract objects. We thus show that these commitments are only ostensible and that the real commitments of our framework are to objects with which we have epistemic contact. In general, then, we cannot allow theories in the basis of our conceptual system which commit us to objects that fail to hook up with our cognitive capacities. Recall that objects are epistemically accessible to us just in case they connect with our cognitive faculties in an empirically scrutable fashion; a theory, we say, is epistemically proximate just in case it commits us to no epistemically inaccessible objects. Ideally, then, we may say that the basis of our conceptual framework must consist solely of epistemically proximate theories. We want, of course, every theory to be epistemically proximate. But the proximity of the basis guarantees this, for reduction is a relative proximity relation, showing that, if the objects to which the reducing theory commits us are epistemically accessible, then so are the objects forced upon us by the reduced theory. Because reducibility relations are transitive and because the basis of the system, by definition, is such that every theory of the system reduces to some theory in the basis, our requirement that the basis contain only epistemically proximate theories guarantees that our system will contain only epistemically proximate theories, for which the dilemma concerning truth does not arise. We thus obtain a criterion for selecting a basis from the set of possible bases of our conceptual scheme: we want a basis containing only epistemically proximate theories.

This, in essence, completes the task of this book. We began by noting that discourse seeming to involve a commitment to abstract objects creates a tension between semantics and epistemology, for it seems that we cannot have any empirically scrutable contact with abstract entities. How can we account for the truth of such discourse, without settling for a metaphor as a theory of knowledge or entirely reconstructing the theory of truth? I have urged that we have only one option: to eliminate reference to abstract objects by eliminating and replacing, by way of ontological reduction, theories that seem to involve commitment to them. I have thus tried to show that we *need* to eliminate reference to abstract objects and then that we can articulate a program for actually performing the elimination. The program is derivational, descending from accounts of reduction as a philosophical, a scientific, and a mathematical tool. Though this theory of reduction is based upon eliminating theories rather than identifying objects, I have shown that we can speak of identities, and other sorts of assertions, in intertheoretic contexts in coherent ways that preserve our usual logical laws and in fact can be supported by a general analysis of the problem of identity. And I have argued that, though Quine rejects a linguistic account of reduction because of the Löwenheim-Skolem theorem, my account allays his fears of a world of numbers without relying on anything akin to proxy functions. Finally, in this chapter, I have developed a theory of ontological commitment. I have distinguished questions of ostensible commitment, closely tied to initial, existential quantification, from questions of real commitment, which take reductive relations into account and which correspond to philosophically interesting matters about what there is. To answer 'What is there?' in a philosophically significant way, it turns out, we must contend with the problem of what there

is *not;* for reductive relations—that is, relations of elimination, of theories and of reference—are crucial to matters of
real commitment. Finally, I have developed an epistemological criterion for making decisions about what we ought to
take as basic in our conceptual scheme. This criterion gives
us a way of making some decisions about what commitments
we ought to count as real, and thus about what answer we
should give to ontology's central question. Of course, being
basic in our conceptual system should correspond with some
intuitive notion of what there *really* is; this is the prime
motivation of the concept. But our best approach to what
there is utilizes the system of knowledge we have developed
about the world in general. We would like, therefore, criteria
that give us the ability to choose some unique candidate from
the set of possible bases of our framework as *the* basis of our
conceptual scheme. If we could do this, there would be nothing to being basic other than satisfying the criteria. So far, of
course, we have only one criterion, which certainly does not
allow us to single out a unique basis for our conceptual system, though it does narrow down the choices.

We thus have an account of how we can show that theories
are epistemically proximate, given that some theories in the
basis are also proximate. But we cannot demonstrate the
proximity of the theories in the basis by way of reduction, for
in general they will reduce to no theory in the system outside
the basis unless mutual reducibility relations are involved.
How else can we demonstrate proximity? The answer, of
course, is that our theories of the acquisition of knowledge
indicate that certain objects are epistemically accessible to
us, in the sense that those theories postulate matter-of-
factual, empirically scrutable relations between us and these
objects. We may take abstract objects as basic, then, and
admit into the basis of our system theories forcing commitments to abstract objects, only if we are willing to recognize
matter-of-factual relations between these entities and persons.[29] Just what relations to our cognitive faculties we
should recognize is, in large part, a matter to be settled not
by philosophers but by cognitive psychologists and
physiologists.

As Michael Dummett has observed, "what objects we recognize the world as containing depends upon the structure of

---

29. Sellars, *Naturalism and Ontology,* p. 16; see also "Empiricism and
Abstract Entities," in Paul A. Schlipp, ed., *The Philosophy of Rudolf Carnap*
(LaSalle, Ill.: Open Court, 1963): 433–468.

our language"(503); it also depends upon the content of our physical and, ultimately, cognitive theories. Ontology may recapitulate philology, but only up to a point. That point is marked by the transition from problems of reducibility, which permit of linguistic treatment, to problems of primacy, which go beyond linguistic matters. The division between reducibility and primacy thus corresponds to the division between linguistic and nonlinguistic problems in ontology.

BIBLIOGRAPHY

Alston, William P. "Ontological Commitments," in Benacerraf and Putnam, cited below: 249–257.

Anderson, Alan Ross. "Church on Ontological Commitment," *Journal of Philosophy*, LVI (1959): 448–451.

Benacerraf, Paul. *Logicism: Some Considerations*. Ph.D. dissertation, Princeton University, 1960.

———. "Mathematical Truth," *Journal of Philosophy*, LXX (1973): 661–679.

———. "What Numbers Could Not Be," *Philosophical Review*, LXXIV (1965): 47–73.

———, and Putnam, Hilary, eds., *Philosophy of Mathematics*. Englewood Cliffs, N.J.: Prentice-Hall, 1964.

Bencivenga, Ermanno. "Are Arithmetical Truths Analytic? New Results in Free Set Theory," *Journal of Philosophical Logic*, VI (1977): 319–330.

Berry, George D. W. "On the Ontological Significance of the Löwenheim-Skolem Theorem," in *Academic Freedom, Logic, and Religion*. Philadelphia: University of Pennsylvania Press, 1953: 39–55.

Carloye, J. C. "Ontological Commitment and Semantics," *Methodology of Science*, X (1977): 169–176.

Carnap, Rudolf. "Empiricism, Semantics, and Ontology," in Benacerraf and Putnam: 233–248.

———. *The Logical Structure of the World*. Translated by R. A. George. Berkeley: University of California Press, 1967.

———. "The Logicist Foundations of Mathematics," in Benacerraf and Putnam: 31–41.

Cartwright, R. L. "Ontology and the Theory of Meaning," *Philosophy of Science*, XXI (1954): 316–325.

Causey, Robert L. "Attribute-identities in Microreductions," *Journal of Philosophy*, LXIX (1972): 407–422.

———. "Identities and Reduction: A Reply," *Noûs*, X (1976): 333–337.

———. "Uniform Microreductions," *Synthese*, XXV (1972): 176–218.

Chateaubriand, Otto. *Ontic Commitment, Ontological Reduction and Ontology*. Ph.D. dissertation, University of California at Berkeley, 1971.

Chihara, Charles S. *Ontology and the Vicious Circle Principle*. Ithaca, N.Y.: Cornell University Press, 1973.

Church, Alonzo. "Ontological Commitment," *Journal of Philosophy*, LV (1958): 1008–1014.

161

Curry, Haskell B. *Foundations of Mathematical Logic*. New York: Dover Publications, 1977.
———. "Remarks on the Definition and Nature of Mathematics," in Benacerraf and Putnam: 152–156.
Dummett, Michael. *Frege: Philosophy of Language*. London: Harper & Row, 1973.
———. "Constructionalism," *Philosophical Review*, LXVI (1957): 47–65.
Feferman, Solomon. "Arithmetization of Metamathematics in a General Setting," *Fundamenta Mathematicae*, XLIX (1960): 35–92.
Feldman, Fred. "Geach and Relative Identity," *Review of Metaphysics*, XXII (1969): 547–555.
———. "A Rejoinder," *Review of Metaphysics*, XXII (1969): 560–561.
Felgner, U. *Models of ZF-Set Theory*. Berlin: Springer-Verlag, 1971.
Feyerabend, Paul K. "Explanation, Reduction, and Empiricism," in Grover Maxwell and Herbert Feigl, eds., *Minnesota Studies in the Philosophy of Sciene*, III. Minneapolis: University of Minnesota Press, 1962.
Geach, Peter. "Identity," *Review of Metaphysics*, XXI (1967): 3–12.
———. *Mental Acts*. New York: Humanities Press, 1957.
———. "Ontological Relativity and Relative Identity," in Milton K. Munitz, ed., *Logic and Ontology*. New York: New York University Press, 1973: 287–302.
———. *Reference and Generality*. Ithaca, N.Y.: Cornell University Press, 1968.
———. "A Reply," *Review of Metaphysics*, XXII (1969): 556–559.
Glymour, Clark. "On Some Patterns of Reduction," *Philosophy of Science*, XXXVII (1970): 340–353.
Gödel, Kurt. "On Formally Undecidable Propositions of *Principia Mathematica* and Related Systems I," in van Heijenoort, cited below: 596–616.
———. "Russell's Mathematical Logic," in Benacerraf and Putnam: 211–232.
———. "What Is Cantor's Continuum Problem?" in Benacerraf and Putnam: 258–273.
Goodman, Nelson. *The Structure of Appearance*. Boston: D. Reidel, 1951, 1977.
———. "A World of Individuals," in Benacerraf and Putnam: 197–210.

Gottlieb, Dale. "Ontological Reduction," *Journal of Philosophy*, LXXIII (1976): 57–76.

Grandy, Richard E. "On What There Need Not Be," *Journal of Philosophy*, LXVI (1969): 809–811.

———. "In Defense of a Modest Platonism," *Philosophical Studies*, XXXII (1977): 359–369.

Hájek, P. "Syntactic Models of Axiomatic Theories," *Bulletin de l'Académie Polonaise des Sciences*, LXXI (1951): 273–278.

Hailperin, T. "Quantification Theory and Empty Individual Domains," *Journal of Symbolic Logic*, XVIII (1953): 197–200.

Harman, Gilbert. "Identifying Numbers," *Analysis*, XXXV (1974): 12.

———. "A Nonessential Property," *Journal of Philosophy*, LXVII (1970): 183–185.

Hart, W. D. "On an Argument for Formalism," *Journal of Philosophy*, LXXI (1974): 29–46.

Hempel, Carl G. "On the Nature of Mathematical Truth," in Benacerraf and Putnam: 366–381.

———. "Reduction: Ontological and Linguistic Facets," in S. Morgenbesser, P. Suppes, and M. White, eds., *Philosophy, Science, and Method*. New York: St. Martin's Press, 1969: 179–199.

———. "Reflections on Nelson Goodman's *The Structure of Appearance*," *Philosophical Review*, LXII (1953): 108–116.

Heyting, Arend. "The Intuitionist Foundations of Mathematics," in Benacerraf and Putnam: 42–49.

Hilbert, David, and Bernays, Paul. *Grundlagen der Mathematik*. Berlin: Springer-Verlag, 1968.

Hochberg, Herbert. "Peano, Russell, and Logicism," in Klemke, cited below: 369–371.

———. "Russell's Reduction of Arithmetic to Logic," in Klemke, cited below: 396–415.

Jubien, Michael. "The Intensionality of Ontological Commitment," *Noûs*, VI (1972): 378–387.

———. "Ontology and Mathematical Truth," *Noûs*, XI (1977): 133–150.

———. "Two Kinds of Reduction," *Journal of Philosophy*, LXVI (1969): 533–541.

Kemeny, John, and Oppenheim, Paul. "On Reduction," *Philosophical Studies*, VII (1956): 6–18.

Kessler, Glenn Paul. *Numbers, Truth, and Knowledge*. Ph.D. dissertation, Princeton University, 1976.

Kitcher, Philip. "The Plight of the Platonist," *Noûs*, XII (1978): 119–136.

Kleene, S. C. *Introduction to Metamathematics*. Groningen: Wolters-Noordhoff Publishing, 1971.

Klemke, E. D., ed., *Essays on Bertrand Russell*. Urbana: University of Illinois Press, 1970.

Kraut, Robert "Indiscernibility and Ontology," *Synthese*, XLIV (1980): 113–135.

———. *Objects*. Ph.D. dissertation, University of Pittsburgh, 1976.

Kreisel, Georg. "Mathematical Significance of Consistency Proofs," *Journal of Symbolic Logic*, XXIII (1958): 155–182.

———. "Models, Translations, and Interpretations," in Thoralf Skolem, ed., *Mathematical Interpretations of Formal Systems*. Amsterdam: North-Holland Publishing, 1955.

———. "On the Concepts of Completeness and Interpretation of Formal Systems," *Fundamenta Mathematicae*, XXXIX (1952): 103–127.

———. "Relative Consistency and Translatability," *Journal of Symbolic Logic*, XXIII (1958): 108–109.

———. "Relative Consistency Proofs," *Journal of Symbolic Logic*, XXIII (1958): 109–110.

Kuhn, Thomas. *The Structure of Scientific Revolutions*. Chicago: University of Chicago Press, 1962.

Lakatos, Imre. *Proofs and Refutations*. Cambridge: Cambridge University Press, 1970.

Lear, Jonathan. "Sets and Semantics," *Journal of Philosophy*, LXXIV (1977): 86–102.

Löwenheim, Leopold. "On Possibilities in the Calculus of Relatives," in van Heijenoort, cited below: 228–251.

Martin, R. M. "On Denotation and Ontic Commitment," *Philosophical Studies*, XIII (1962): 35–38.

Massey, Gerald J. *The Philosophy of Space*. Ph.D. dissertation, Princeton University, 1963.

———. "Reflections on the Unity of Science," *Annals of the Japanese Association for the Philosophy of Science*, IV (1973): 1–19.

Mostowski, A. "On the Rules of Proof in the Pure Functional Calculus of the First Order," *Journal of Symbolic Logic*, XVI (1951): 107–111.

Motohashi, Nobuyoshi. "Partially Ordered Interpretations," *Journal of Symbolic Logic*, XLII (1977): 83–93.

Mycielski, Jan. "A Lattice Connected with Relative Interpretability Types of Theories," *Notices of the Mathematical Society*, IX (1962): 407–408; errata, XVIII (1971): 984.

———. "A Lattice of Interpretability Types of Theories," *Journal of Symbolic Logic*, XLII (1977): 297–305.

Myhill, John. "On the Ontological Significance of the Löwenheim-Skolem Theorem," in *Academic Freedom, Logic, and Religion*. Philadelphia: University of Pennsylvania Press, 1953: 57–70.

Nagel, Ernest. "Issues in the Logic of Reductive Explanations," in Howard Kiefer and Milton Munitz, eds., *Mind, Science, and History*. Albany: State University of New York Press, 1970.

———. *The Structure of Science*. Indianapolis: Hackett Publishing Co., 1979.

Nelson, Jack. "On the Alleged Incompleteness of Certain Identity Claims," *Canadian Journal of Philosophy*, III (1973): 105–113.

———. "Relative Identity," *Noûs*, IV (1970): 241–260.

Nickles, Thomas. "Two Concepts of Intertheoretic Reduction," *Journal of Philosophy*, LXX (1973): 181–201.

Perry, John. "The Same *F*," *Philosophical Review*, LXXIX (1970): 181–200.

Pollock, J. L. "On Logicism," in Klemke: 388–395.

Popper, Karl R. "The Aim of Science," *Ratio*, I (1957): 24–35.

———. *Conjectures and Refutations*. New York: Basic Books, 1962.

Quine, Willard van Orman. *From a Logical Point of View*. New York: Harper & Row, 1961.

———. "Identity," mimeographed.

———. *Ontological Relativity and Other Essays*. New York: Columbia University Press, 1969.

———. "Ontology and Ideology," *Philosophical Studies*, II (1951): 11–15.

———. "Russell's Ontological Development," in Klemke: 3–14.

———. *Selected Logic Papers*. New York: Random House, 1966.

———. *The Ways of Paradox and Other Essays*. Cambridge, Mass.: Harvard University Press, 1976.

———. *Word and Object*. Cambridge, Mass.: MIT Press, 1960.

Reichenbach, Hans. "Bertrand Russell's Logic," in Schilpp, cited below: 21–54.

Resnick, Michael David. "The Frege-Hilbert Controversy," *Philosophy and Phenomenological Research*, XXXIV (1974): 386–403.

————. "Mathematical Knowledge and Pattern Cognition," *Canadian Journal of Philosophy*, V (1975): 25–39.

Robbins, Beverly. "Ontology and the Hierarchy of Languages," *Philosophical Review*, LXVII (1958): 531–537.

Russell, Bertrand. *Essays in Analysis*. Edited by D. Lackey. New York: George Braziller, 1973.

————. *Introduction to Mathematical Philosophy*. London: George Allen & Unwin, 1919.

————. *Logic and Knowledge*. Edited by Robert C. Marsh. New York: G. P. Putnam's Sons, 1956.

————. "My Mental Development," in Schilpp, cited below: 1–20.

————. *The Principles of Mathematics*. New York: W. W. Norton & Company, 1903.

Schaffner, Kenneth F. "Approaches to Reduction," *Philosophy of Science*, XXXIV (1967): 137–147.

Schilpp, Paul Arthur, ed., *The Philosophy of Bertrand Russell*. Evanston, Ill.: The Library of Living Philosophers V, 1946.

Sellars, Wilfrid. "Abstract Entities," *Review of Metaphysics*, XVI (1963): reprinted in *Philosophical Perspectives*. Springfield, Ill.: Charles C Thomas, 1967: 229–269.

————. "Empiricism and Abstract Entities," in Paul Arthur Schilpp, ed., *The Philosophy of Rudolf Carnap*. LaSalle, Ill.: Open Court, 1963: 433–468; reprinted in *Essays in Philosophy and Its History*. Boston: D. Reidel, 1974: 245–286.

————. "Mind, Meaning, and Behavior," *Philosophical Studies*, III (1952): 83–95.

————. *Naturalism and Ontology*. Reseda, Calif.: Ridgeview Publishing Company, 1979.

————. "On the Introduction of Abstract Entities," in B. Freed, A. Marras, and P. Maynard, eds., *Forms of Representation*. Amsterdam: North-Holland Publishing, 1975: 47–74. Reprinted in *Essays in Philosophy and Its History*: 287–317.

————. *Philosophical Perspectives*. Springfield, Ill.: Charles C Thomas, 1967.

————. *Science, Perception and Reality*. London: Routledge & Kegan Paul, 1963.

Shoemaker, Sydney. "Wiggins on Identity," *Philosophical Review*, LXXIX (1970): 529–544.

Sicha, Jeffrey. "Logic: The Fundamentals of a Sellarsian Theory," in Joseph C. Pitt, ed., *The Philosophy of Wilfrid*

Sellars: Queries and Extensions. Boston: D. Reidel, 1978: 257–286.

Sklar, Lawrence. "Types of Intertheoretic Reduction," *British Journal for the Philosophy of Science*, XVIII (1967): 109–124.

Skolem, Thoralf. "Logico-combinatorial Investigations in the Satisfiability or Provability of Mathematical Propositions: A Simplified Proof of a Theorem by L. Löwenheim and Generalizations of the Theorem," in van Heijenoort, cited below: 252–263.

Steiner, Mark. *Mathematical Knowledge.* Ithaca, N.Y.: Cornell University Press, 1975.

———. "Mathematics, Explanation, and Scientific Knowledge," *Noûs*, XII (1978): 17–28.

Stevenson, Leslie. "Extensional and Intensional Logic for Criteria of Identity," *Logique et Analyse*, XX (1977): 268–285.

———. "On What Sorts of Thing There Are," *Mind*, LXXXV (1976): 503–521.

———. "Relative Identity and Leibniz's Law," *Philosophical Quarterly*, XXII (1972): 155–158.

Strawson, Peter F. "On Referring," in Jay Rosenberg and Charles Travis, eds., *Readings in the Philosophy of Language.* Englewood Cliffs, N.J.: Prentice-Hall, 1971: 175–194.

Suppes, Patrick. *Introduction to Logic.* Princeton, N.J.: Van Nostrand, 1957.

Swanson, J. W. "On the Kemeny-Oppenheim Treatment of Reduction," *Philosophical Studies*, XIII (1962): 94–96.

Szczerba, L. W. "Interpretability of Elementary Theories," in R. Butts and J. Hintikka, eds., *Logic, Foundations of Mathematics, and Computability Theory.* Boston: D. Reidel, 1977: 129–145.

Tarski, Alfred, Mostowski, A., and Robinson, R. M. *Undecidable Theories.* Amsterdam: North-Holland Publishing, 1953.

Tharp, Leslie. "Myth and Mathematics," mimeographed.

———. "Ontological Reduction," *Journal of Philosophy*, LXVIII (1971): 151–164.

van Fraassen, Bas. "The Completeness of Free Logic," *Zeitschrift für Mathematische Logik und Grundlagen der Mathematik*, XII (1966): 219–234.

———. *Formal Semantics and Logic.* New York: Macmillan, 1971.

———. "Singular Terms, Truth-value Gaps, and Free Logic," *Journal of Philosophy*, LXIII (1966): 481–495.

van Heijenoort, Jean, ed., *From Frege to Gödel: A Sourcebook in Mathematical Logic, 1879–1931*. Cambridge, Mass.: Harvard University Press, 1967.

Wang, Hao. *A Survey of Mathematical Logic*. Peking: Science Press, 1963.

Whitehead, Alfred North, and Russell, Bertrand. *Principia Mathematica to *56*. Cambridge: Cambridge University Press, 1962.

Zemach, Eddy M. "In Defense of Relative Identity," *Philosophical Studies*, xxvi (1974): 207–218.

INDEX

Abstract entities
  and Benacerraf's dilemma, 9, 10,
    13, 14, 19, 156
  and contensivism, 10, 11
  and convention, 94
  counterfactuals concerning,
    55–56, 59
  epistemic contact with, 5, 11,
    13–14, 18, 133–34
  and extensionality, 38, 50–51
  and multiple reducibility, 77–78
  nonmathematical, 13, 45, 51
  and ontic decision, 156–58
  and reduction, 3–4, 133–34, 151
  reference to, 3–5
  in scientific theories, 45, 50–52,
    54–56
  vs. physical objects, 13–14, 94,
    127
Alien implications, 131–32
Ambiguity
  of intertheoretic sentences, 84,
    93
  of reference, 108–110
  of semantic ambiguity, 111–12
Amplified arithmetics, 121–24, 128
Analyticity, 30, 47, 51
Approximation, 52–54, 100
Argument from possibility of revision, 96–103, 107
Arithmetic, 9, 16, 18, 24, 134
  and arithmetical truth, 58, 118,
    130
  and neo-Pythagoreanism, 114–
    15, 118, 120–22, 128
  Peano, 24, 71n, 75, 77, 119–21
  Presburger, 38–39, 115, 119–20
  relation to set theory of, 16,
    35–41, 45, 56, 68–69, 77–82,
    91–92, 118, 122–23, 128,
    146–56
  Robinson, 115, 119–20
Arithmetical definability, 75,
  121–24, 128
Arithmetization, 63, 71n, 75, 118,
  120–23, 128

Assignment function, 87–88
Assumption one, 8, 10–11, 17–18
Assumption two, 8–9, 11, 17–18
Axiomatic Theories, 58, 121–23

Background language, 150–52
Basic objects, 29, 31, 98–99,
  155–58
Basis
  of constructional system, 31, 66,
    67, 156
  of cumulative hierarchy, 40
  and epistemic proximity, 156–58
  and ontic decision, 155–58
  possible, 155-57
Benacerraf, Paul, 3, 7–13, 26,
  77–78, 80–86, 91–93, 156
Benacerraf's dilemma
  and abstract entities, 13–14, 156
  generalized, 8–9, 13–14, 17–19
  and mathematical truth, 7–8,
    12–13
  strategies for resolving, 17–19
Berry, G. D. W., 126
Bivalence, 89–91
Bourbaki, N., 22
Bridge laws. See Connecting assumptions.

"Canadian mountie" theory, 9, 11,
  14, 18
Cantor, Georg, 143
Carnap, Rudolf, 4, 17, 21, 27,
  30–34, 37, 41–45, 59, 66, 70–72,
  85, 133, 135, 146, 148, 154
Causey, Robert L., 51–52
Chateaubriand, Otto, 148
Chihara, Charles, 116, 127, 148
Church, Alonzo, 62n, 136
Cognitive science, 5, 8, 133–34,
  158–59
Cohen, Paul J., 61
Colorese, 99–102, 106, 109
Completeness
  and axiomatizability, 121
  and bivalence, 90

169